T0322561

THE OFFICIAL
GUINNESS
COOKBOOK

OVER **70** RECIPES FOR
COOKING AND BAKING FROM
IRELAND'S FAMOUS BREWERY

THE OFFICIAL
GUINNESS
COOKBOOK

CAROLINE
HENNESSY

PHOTOGRAPHY BY EVI ABELER

**TITAN
BOOKS**

LONDON

CONTENTS

INTRODUCTION

Magic in a glass. That's what a Guinness beer is.
On one level, Guinness could simply be described as a brand of Irish stout. But don't be fooled; that doesn't even come close to summing it up. Guinness is an Irish icon, it's a 262-year-old—and counting!—brewery, it's the story of a vision, it's an advertising star.

It's a moment of pure perfection.

When it comes down to it, Guinness beers are beverages that are made to be enjoyed responsibly with friends, along with some good food. They are also, as many home cooks have discovered, incredibly successful when incorporated into some good food. Now, with this cookbook, you'll be able to discover the joy of cooking with Guinness for yourself. Whether whipping up a quick batch of soda bread for your family or creating an impressive dinner party for friends, this book has you covered with recipes for dishes, baked goods, and even cocktails featuring the stouts, ales, and lagers of the Guinness Breweries from around the world.

Learning a little helps you to appreciate what's in your glass. Before you begin cooking, go back to the beginning and discover the history of Guinness, how it is made, and why it stands out from the crowd. Although we may already understand how important it is to take time to savor a pint, this book brings that experience to another level with a few tips on pairing Guinness beers with food. Explore tasting notes for Guinness Draught, Guinness Extra Stout, Guinness Foreign Extra Stout, and more, and learn how to properly taste and pair the beers. Then discover how to maximize all those complex flavors with a range of beer-friendly cooking techniques and ingredients. These are the basics of cooking with Guinness. Once you've mastered them, you're ready to move on to the recipes.

From old favorites (Traditional Beef and Guinness Stew, page 72) to modern show-stoppers (Groundnut Chicken and Sweet Potato Stew With Foreign Extra Stout, page 81) to recipes from the Guinness Storehouse in Dublin and the Open Gate Brewery in Baltimore, this book is all about having your Guinness beer and eating it too. We hope it brings you as much joy as a quiet pint at the end of a long day.

Sláinte!

ALL ABOUT GUINNESS

A BRIEF HISTORY OF ARTHUR GUINNESS

Born in 1725, Arthur Guinness had a vision. An ambitious young man with a £100 inheritance in his pocket, he embarked on his career in 1756 by setting up a small brewery in Leixlip, County Kildare. It wasn't an easy time for Irish brewers; taxes on beer were constantly changing to favor first one party then another. But Arthur didn't let that stop him. In 1759, he left the Leixlip brewery to his younger brother, Richard, and headed for Dublin, which was in the process of rapid transformation from the high walls and narrow winding alleys of the medieval period into the gracious houses and wide streets of a Georgian city that are still evident today.

An astute businessman, Arthur acquired a closed brewery on the southern banks of the River Liffey. The four acres of the former St. James's Gate Brewery—which included a brewhouse, mill, malthouses, stables for twelve brewery horses, and a hayloft—became his property for a downpayment of £100 and a rent of £45 a year. St. James's Gate was ideally located at the center of what was to become a major transport hub over the next century. Barges on the Grand Canal brought barley into Dublin from the countryside and took beer back out, barges on the Liffey transported Guinness to meet Guinness-owned ships at the Dublin docks, and a link to the Irish rail network terminus at Heuston Station meant that freight trains could take casks of Guinness all around Ireland.

But that was all to come. On December 31, 1759, Arthur took a wild leap of ambitious faith and signed a lease for nine thousand years.

Arthur initially started brewing ale at St. James's Gate, but he had his eye on quite another kind of beer. In the 1770s, a strong dark beer called porter, initially brewed in London and adopted as the beer of choice by the market porters of Covent Garden and Billingsgate, was being imported into Ireland and becoming increasingly popular. By 1796, brewery records note that much more porter than ale was being brewed at St. James's Gate, and by 1799, Arthur had switched to brewing porter full-time. This proved to be a shrewd move, as it was porter that would eventually take Guinness from a small Dublin brewery to a major international brand.

OPPOSITE: Portrait of Arthur Guinness (1725-1803). ABOVE: A 19th century lithograph depicting St. James's Gate Brewery.

By the 1830s, thirty years after Arthur's death, St. James's Gate had become the largest brewery in Ireland, with Guinness beer being exported to England, the United States, the Caribbean, and West Africa. West India Porter, the precursor of Guinness Foreign Extra Stout, was brewed for the overseas market while Guinness Extra Superior Porter, the forerunner of Guinness Extra Stout, was for consumption in Ireland and Great Britain. No matter where you were in the world, Guinness quality control was paramount. In the 1890s, the company even appointed overseas travelers to keep an eye on product quality. It's this kind of attention to detail that has made Guinness, in all formats, such a superior and consistent beer.

As for Arthur, while making his mark as a brewer, the savvy businessman also found time to get married—to Dublin heiress Olivia Whitmore in 1761. Olivia subsequently gave birth to twenty-one children, ten of which survived into adulthood. Three of their sons worked in the business with Arthur, while Arthur himself was active in the business until his seventies.

By the time Arthur Guinness died in 1803 at the age of 78, he was a prosperous and well-known Dublin businessman. Having embarked on his brewing venture with just £100, he died with a large personal fortune of about £23,000 and a flourishing business that would continue to grow and succeed under his family's stewardship.

GUINNESS: A TIMELINE

1759 Arthur Guinness signs a nine-thousand-year lease for £45 a year on a closed brewery at St. James's Gate in Dublin.

1799 The end of ale. Guinness decides to concentrate solely on brewing porter.

1801 West India Porter, the ancestor of today's Guinness Foreign Extra Stout, is first brewed.

1803 Founder Arthur Guinness dies. The brewery is taken over by his son, Arthur Guinness II.

1817 The first shipment of Guinness beer arrives in the United States, delivered to a port in South Carolina.

1821 Arthur Guinness II records instructions for brewing Guinness Extra Superior Porter, the forerunner of modern-day Guinness Extra Stout.

1833 The brewery has survived the post-Napoleonic Wars recession to become the largest brewery in Ireland.

1837 Benjamin Disraeli (British prime minister from 1874 to 1880) records in a letter his encounter with oysters and Guinness.

1855 Arthur Guinness II dies. His son Sir Benjamin Lee Guinness takes over the brewery.

1862 The trademark beer label—a buff oval label with Arthur Guinness's signature, still used on Guinness products today—is introduced.

1868 Benjamin Lee Guinness dies. His son Edward Cecil Guinness takes over the business, doubling the size of the brewery.

1877 A fleet of specially designed barges are commissioned to transport Guinness barrels along the River Liffey.

ABOVE: An early advertisement for Guinness Extra Stout.

1886 Guinness—the largest brewery in the world—becomes the first major brewery to be floated on the London Stock Exchange.

1927 Rupert Guinness, eldest son of Edward Cecil Guinness, becomes chairman.

1929 The first advertisement for Guinness is created.

1936 Guinness opens its first overseas brewery at Park Royal, London, to supply stout to England.

1959 Guinness celebrates its 200th anniversary. Guinness Draught is introduced as the world's first nitro beer.

1963 The first bottle of Guinness Foreign Extra Stout is brewed in Nigeria, the site of the first overseas brewery outside Ireland and the UK.

1988 The Guinness widget—a device to nitrogenate Guinness in cans—is developed. It wins the Queen's Award for Technological Achievement in 1991.

2000 The Guinness Storehouse—a former fermentation plant—is opened at the St. James's Gate Brewery, becoming the official home of Guinness in the historic heart of Dublin.

2014 An updated production facility, Brewhouse 4, is opened at St. James's Gate. The largest stout brewery in the world, it is also one of the most technologically advanced and environmentally sustainable breweries ever built.

2015 The Open Gate Brewery in Dublin, "the home of innovation at Guinness," opens to the public. Alongside Guinness Draught, the taproom features limited edition experimental brews from the pilot brewery.

2018 The Open Gate Brewery opens in Baltimore, Maryland. With a focus on innovation and experimentation, particularly in the area of barrel-aging, the brewery combines Irish brewing expertise and American beer creativity. Hop House 13 is the brewery's flagship beer.

WHEN PORTER BECOMES STOUT

Guinness started exclusively brewing porter, a dark English style of beer, in 1799. Around 1810, Guinness started to brew a stronger beer, a "stouter kind of porter," and over time this became known simply as stout.

GUINNESS GOES NITRO

When you order a pint of Guinness Draught in a pub, it has a thick, creamy, deliciously distinctive head and exceptionally smooth mouthfeel. This innovation, which came about in 1959, comes from using nitrogen gas to give Guinness that creamy head. When it came to canning Guinness Draught, the brewers came up with another bright idea. It's a simple widget—you'll hear it knocking around in the bottom of your can—that uses a nitrogen-filled capsule that is released when the can is opened. Pour and admire that glorious pint.

WHAT'S IN A GLASS?

Guinness beer is made from four ingredients.

BARLEY

Hold a glass of Guinness Draught up to the light. Although the beer might be known colloquially as the "black stuff," when you take a proper look, you can see that it's actually a deep shade of ruby red. The reason for this is roasted barley—it gives the beer its deep red color and distinctively rich, bitter roasted flavor.

Guinness beer uses three kinds of barley: unmalted barley, malted barley (also called malt), and roasted barley. Freshly milled malted barley gives the beer body and sweet malty flavors, while the roasted barley contributes the dry coffee-ish flavor and deep ruby color that are characteristic of Guinness. The roasting takes place on site, with unmalted barley heated to 449.6°F (232°C) in large drums that resemble coffee bean roasters.

TOP: Interior view of No. 2 Brewhouse, 1948.
ABOVE: Racking casks of Guinness Stout on the Racking Floor at St. James's Gate Brewery, 1906.

HOPS

Hops, the flowers of a perennial plant, are essential in brewing. Along with the flavor, aroma, and bitterness they contribute, hops also act as a natural preservative. In Guinness, the hop bitterness offers a balance to the sweet roasted flavors of the malt.

YEAST

Without yeast, Guinness would be missing an essential element: alcohol. Yeast converts the natural sugars extracted from the barley into alcohol and carbon dioxide, developing the characteristic Guinness flavor in the process. The proprietary yeast used for brewing Guinness has been used by several generations of brewers.

WATER

Historically, St. James's Gate Brewery used water that came from the headwaters of the River Liffey, at Poulaphouca Reservoir in the Wicklow Mountains. This source supplied soft water that had mineral content suitable for stout brewing. Today, the brewers obtain water from other local water suppliers and, thanks to modern advances in brewing, treat the water by adding the right amount of brewing salts and other minerals back in, thus creating the perfect quality water for each beer type.

ABOVE: Brewery workers skim off excess yeast at Market Street Storehouse at St. James's Gate Brewery, 1906.
ABOVE RIGHT: Barley spread across malting floor in Cooke's Lane Maltings at St. James's Gate Brewery, 1950–1955.

GUINNESS AND FOOD

WHY PAIR GUINNESS WITH FOOD?

Go anywhere in the world and you're likely to find a Guinness beer. There's a dark pint of creamy stout waiting for you in the most unexpected spots, from Kuala Lumpur to Lagos to Kansas City. By itself, the beer is a true pleasure, but when you take this familiar delight and put it together with food, you're in for a most unexpected treat. Quite simply, Guinness brings food to another level.

HOT POT
Hodge Podge or Hotch Potch—no-one agrees on the name. Sir Kenelme Digby clouds the issue still more with his "Hotch-pot". Tastiest of all is a Lancashire version made from mutton, kidneys, mushrooms and oysters—an exceptional excuse for Guinness.

CORNISH PASTIES
are exactly described in an old Cornish rhyme : "Pastry rolled out like a plate, Piled with turmut, tates and mate, Doubled up and baked like fate". What makes a Cornish Pasty so distinguished is that the filling starts raw and cooks in its own juices.

GUINNESS GOES WELL WITH GOOD FOOD
Naturally good in itself, it adds goodness to any good meal.

There's a very special synergy between beer and food that can elevate the moment, turning a simple meal into something altogether more memorable. Pay a little attention to what's in your glass and on your plate, and when you hit the right pairing, you're in for a transcendent moment.

This focus on food is nothing new. From the late 1920s, Guinness and food was a popular advertising theme. Advertisements from the 1950s offer pairing ideas for fish, cheese, curry, lamb, steak, and Christmas food. The advertisements all had the same simple, effective message: "Guinness goes well with good food."

ABOVE: Excerpt from "Guinness Guide to Country Dishes," 1950s.

ESSENTIAL PRINCIPLES FOR PAIRING BEER AND FOOD:

a. Balance: When pairing beer and food, it's essential to have balance; one shouldn't overpower the other. When looking for a beer to go with delicate dishes, like a summer salad or steamed fish, Hop House 13 or Baltimore Blonde won't overwhelm the flavors. Richer meals—a slow-cooked beef stew, for instance—need more heft, and this is where the darker, full-bodied stouts come in.

b. Cut: Unlike wine, beer has the ability to cut through the texture and flavor of food. Carbonation is its secret weapon. Spicy, deep-fried, or fatty foods don't stand a chance against the cutting power of these bubbles, which cleanse your mouth with each sip so you can really taste the food. The bitterness of hops and roasted barley is another weapon in beer's particular arsenal, cutting through rich dishes. The traditional Irish pub lunch of creamy seafood chowder works well with Guinness Draught for that exact reason.

c. Complement: For a complementary beer and food pairing, you're looking to match similar flavors and aromas. Play with the citrus flavors of Hop House 13 by drinking it alongside Hop House 13 Lime Fish Tacos (page 93) or take the full-bodied malty notes of Guinness Extra Stout, pair it with a dark chocolate dessert, and observe how the flavors sing together.

d. Contrast: A contrasting pairing is all about highlighting opposing flavors. To use the same beer, Guinness Extra Stout can act as a brilliant counterpoint to savory flavors, letting them shine. Pair the beer with a blue cheese and see how it enhances the salty funk of the cheese. Think about Guinness Draught and freshly shucked oysters: a classic contrast.

e. Seasonality: Certain drinks and foods appeal at different times. Hot summer weather has us reaching for brighter ales and lagers, like Hop House 13 or Baltimore Blonde, to pair with salads and barbecue; when dark winter nights draw in, we stick closer to the fire and concentrate on heavier stouts that go with rich dishes like stews, casseroles, and Christmas pudding.

THE ART OF TASTING

STORING

Most cans and bottles of beer are meant to be enjoyed sooner rather than later, maybe even as soon as you get them home! Always keep an eye on best-before dates, make sure to store the bottles and cans out of the light in a cool place, and don't leave your beer sitting around for too long (unless it's meant to be aged).

SERVING

If beer is too cold, you can't taste much of the flavor that the brewer has been working hard to get into your glass. Check the beer can or bottle for suitable serving temperatures.

Guinness Draught:
42.8°F (6°C)

Guinness Extra Stout:
50°F (10°C)

Guinness Foreign Extra Stout:
50° to 55°F (10° to 12.7°C)

Over the Moon Milk Stout:
47° to 50°F (7° to 10°C)

Hop House 13:
37.4° to 41°F (3° to 5°C)

Hop House 13:
37.4° to 41°F (3° to 5°C)

GLASSWARE

Does a glass actually make a difference? Yes, it certainly does! You always want to serve beer in a glass so that you can properly see, taste, and enjoy it. There are certainly times when nothing but a pint glass will do. If, however, you want to spend a bit more time with your beer, go for a simple stemmed tulip-style beer glass, which lets you do a bit more swirling, sniffing, and savoring.

THE GUINNESS PERFECT POUR

Pouring the perfect pint is a skill that has to be learned. If you're in a pub, the "two-part pour" takes 119.53 seconds and a little bit of patience. The first pour, at a 45-degree angle, fills the glass three-quarters of the way. After this pour settles, the server fills the glass to the top and hands over the distinctive black pint with its creamy white head. It's something that pubs take enormous pride in, and there are many debates to be had over the spot for a perfect pint!

At home, it's a little simpler. Start with a large, clean, dry glass and a chilled can or bottle. Tilt the glass at a 45-degree angle and pour the Guinness all at once in one smooth action. Allow the beer to settle, then enjoy responsibly.

"Nine out of ten GUINNESS drinkers can tell how good a pint is by how you present it to them"
GIG Consumer Planning Research

GUINNESS DRAUGHT

6 Steps to Perfection

GUINNESS The most natural thing in the world.

ABOVE: Press advertisement showing the six steps to pouring the perfect pint, as advertised in the Licensing World Trade Directory, 2002.

HOW TO TASTE

ABOVE: Visitors' Sample Room at St. James's Gate Brewery, 1906.

I. LOOK

After pouring your beer into a proper glass, hold it up to the light and take a good look at the color, clarity, and carbonation. What color is it? Golden, amber, or an intense ruby red? Note the beer's clarity—it could be dark and opaque or clear and sparkling. What kind of head does it have? You also want to watch out for carbonation: lots of bubbles or just a few? The visual impact of a beer makes a big difference in how you experience it, so take a few minutes at this stage to appreciate what's in your glass.

2. SWIRL AND SNIFF

Like wine, you need to get your nose into a glass of beer to get the measure of what you're drinking. Gently—you don't want to spill it all over yourself!— swirl the beer in the glass and inhale the aroma. Pay attention to what your nose is telling you: Smell plays an enormous part in what we perceive as flavor, so this step gives you an idea of what the beer will taste like. Watch out for bright hop aromas (citrus, pine, herbs) and the deeper bass notes of malt (bread, toast, chocolate, coffee).

3. SIP

Finally! Take a well-earned sip of that beer and savor it. Are the flavors that you're experiencing chiming in with the aromas that you identified earlier? As the beer warms up in your mouth, the flavors of hops and malt gradually unfold, giving you a new perspective on what you're tasting. When you swallow—never spit!—the full hit of bitterness comes through on the palate, which is an essential part of tasting. What kind of overall impression are you getting? How does it feel in your mouth? Take note of the texture, body, carbonation, and creaminess.

4. AFTERTASTE

What's your final impression of the beer? The flavors and aromas that linger on the palate are an important part of a beer's drinkability and likeability. Most important, this is when you decide if you want another sip.

TASTING NOTES

Guinness Draught Stout

ABV: 4.2%

Aroma: Hints of roasted coffee and chocolate.

Flavor: Smoothly balanced with bitter, sweet, and roasted notes.

Palate: Smooth, creamy, and balanced.

Appearance: Dark ruby red, with a creamy head.

Guinness Extra Stout

ABV: 5.6%

Aroma: Subtly fruity with warming, roasted notes of coffee and dark chocolate.

Flavor: Crisp and balanced with bitter, sweet, roasted notes and a dry finish.

Palate: Smooth with a slight bite leading to a dry finish.

Appearance: Dark ruby red with a frothy head.

Guinness Foreign Extra Stout

ABV: 7.5%

Aroma: Robust and roasted with intense notes of dark chocolate, caramel, and dried fruits.

Flavor: Full-bodied with coffee notes balanced with subtle sweetness

Palate: Initial tingling impact, bittersweet leading to a dry finish.

Appearance: Black liquid with a frothy head

Guinness Over the Moon Milk Stout

ABV: 5.3%

Aroma: Espresso and chocolate.

Flavor: Cocoa, caramel, fresh coffee, and sweet fruit.

Palate: Smooth, finishing with a hint of sweetness.

Appearance: Deep brown but clear beer with a white head.

Brewed in Baltimore's Open Gate Brewery. Mostly available in the United States.

Guinness Baltimore Blonde

ABV: 5%

Aroma: Clean, hoppy character with floral and citrus notes.

Flavor: Complex, malty notes and hoppy character with a refreshing and bitter finish.

Palate: Lively mouthfeel; crisp and refreshing with a long malty, biscuity finish.

Appearance: Golden amber color with a dense head.

Brewed in Baltimore's Open Gate Brewery. Mostly available in the United States.

Guinness Hop House 13 Lager

ABV: 5%

Aroma: Sweet and fruity with hints of apricot and peach.

Flavor: Crisp, full-flavored, and refreshing; hoppy, but not too buttery with a malty finish.

Palate: Lively palate; crisp and refreshing taste.

Appearance: Golden, bright, and clear.

Brewed in Dublin's St. James's Gate Brewery. Mostly available in Ireland, the United Kingdom, and Europe.

PERFECT PAIRS

Guinness Draught Stout: Chargrilled vegetables, short ribs, smoked salmon, oysters, mature cheddar, blackberry tart.

Guinness Extra Stout: Roasted garlic hummus, chorizo, grilled oysters, crab crème brûlée, baked Brie with honey and thyme, brownies, vanilla ice cream.

Guinness Foreign Extra Stout: Whole baked celeriac, lobster rolls, venison stew, blue cheese, flourless dark chocolate and cherry cake, tiramisu.

Guinness Over the Moon Milk Stout: Moroccan vegetable tagine, Puebla-style turkey mole, salted peanuts, Gouda cheese, chocolate chip cookies, vanilla ice cream.

Guinness Hop House 13: Spiced roasted cauliflower, bratwurst, nachos and salsa, buffalo wings, ceviche, mild cheddar, New York cheesecake.

Guinness Hop House 13 Lager: Brown-butter popcorn, pulled jackfruit bao, pizza, jerk chicken, fresh goat cheese, lemon delicious pudding.

ABOVE: Food-themed press advertisements for Guinness stout, 1957.

GUINNESS IN FOOD

WHY COOK WITH GUINNESS?

Guinness is an integral part of Irish cuisine, with many a glass of stout bypassing the cook and instead ending up in a stew or fruitcake. Traditional Beef and Guinness Stew (page 72) has long been a mainstay, both of home cooking and as an Irish pub food offering, and everyone's Irish granny has their own particular recipe for porter cake (for the official one, see page 102). Although traditional recipes like these are always appreciated, one should never be afraid of pushing the envelope. Adding Guinness to your repertoire of ingredients brings a slew of new, complex flavors to the pot: the dark bitter, roasted, and toasty notes in Guinness Draught and Guinness Extra Stout; the deep richness of Foreign Extra Stout; the lighter, refreshingly bitter hops of Hop House 13 or Baltimore Blonde. All of these have their parts to play on the cooking stage. Adding Guinness to a recipe can be as simple as substituting it for wine or stock or as elaborate as taking the time to make a Harissa-Beer Butter (page 79) or multilayered Foreign Extra Stout Barbecue Sauce (page 63). The possibilities are endless.

Innovation and experimentation with Guinness in food is nothing new. In the Guinness Archive, there are copies of recipe booklets from 1954 that were distributed to publicans, some of which feature Guinness as an ingredient in dishes like kidneys in Guinness, Christmas pudding, and salami of game. Recipes from a Guinness stout cooking competition at the Culinary Institute of America in 1983 include Guinness cheese phyllo triangles, chicken Guinnessto, stout pumpernickel soup, and a rich creamy shrimp stout—the overall winner that day.

Copies of other cooking and baking pamphlets held in the Guinness archives include—alongside the expected stews, casseroles, cakes, and plum puddings—recipes for fricassée de lapin (rabbit fricassée), figs with Guinness, a gelatin mold mixed fruit special, and a savory mushroom and Guinness cheesecake. These official recipe sheets were sent out to customers who wrote in and requested them, demonstrating, firstly, that people love putting beer in their food and, secondly, that Guinness has always been happy to help them push culinary boundaries.

HOW TO COOK WITH GUINNESS

Like having a Guinness with your food? Then you're going to love using it in your cooking!

There's a very special alchemy that happens when you add a brew to the pot. The dark stouts have complex barley and malt flavors that deepen and amplify the flavor of meats and baked goods, while lighter ales and lagers have hops to add a welcome edge of bitterness to cheesy or sweet foods.

Why not have a Guinness beer in your glass and on your plate?

TIPS AND NOTES FOR COOKING WITH BEER

- Use freshly opened beer at room temperature.
- Open the beer and pour it into a glass, letting it rest a few minutes before you need to measure it so that the head dissipates and some of the carbonation is released.
- The easiest way to measure beer is on a digital scale that measures milliliters. Need 120ml of beer for a recipe? Just weigh it out.
- When you cook with beer, some—but not all—of the alcohol evaporates while the flavor remains, depending on the temperature and duration of cooking. Please add beer responsibly to your favorite meals.
- Stick with full-fat dairy products. The acid in beer can curdle the low-fat kinds.

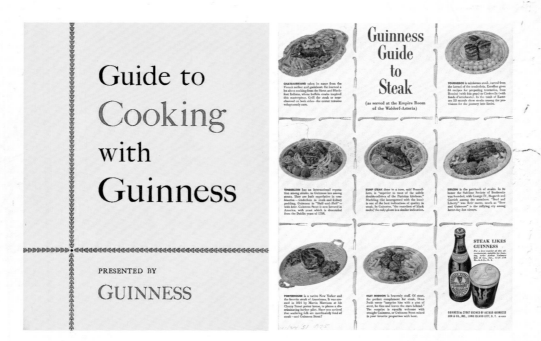

ABOVE: "Guinness Guide to Steak" recipe leaflet issued to customers, 1950s.

BEER-FRIENDLY COOKING TECHNIQUES

1. STEAMING

Seafood steamed in beer is a classic for a good reason: The natural sweetness of shellfish is balanced by the gentle bitterness of a lager or ale. One taste of mussels or clams steamed with Hop House 13 or Baltimore Blonde and you'll know why (see Steamed Mussels in Hop House 13, page 88). Beer-can chicken may look somewhat undignified, but no one will be laughing when they taste the succulent meat that results from a cooking method that infuses the flavors of Guinness via steam (see Sticky, Spicy Beer Can Chicken, page 82).

2. MARINATING

The simplest way of introducing beer to your food is probably a marinade. Beer is acidic, so it makes the perfect marinade base. Even an hour's worth of marinating will add flavor and moisture to your meat or fish. The trick is to balance the beer and the ingredients: Hop House 13 and Baltimore Blonde work best in light, zesty marinades for fish, shrimp, chicken, and pork. Guinness Draught and Extra Stout work well in more earthy marinades for lamb and beef. Guinness Foreign Extra Stout can take on game meat like boar and venison.

3. SAUCES AND CONDIMENTS

The flavors in Guinness can also act as a seasoning, enhancing sauces, vinaigrettes, mustards, jams, and relishes. Stout's malt notes play nicely with the spice of a homemade mustard (see Chile Extra Stout Mustard, page 62), while Hop House 13 or Baltimore Blonde complements lime and chile in a grain salad (see Squash, Spinach, and Barley Salad With Hop House 13 Chile-Lime Dressing, page 61).

4. IN BATTER

Adding beer to batter is an old gastropub trick that imparts flavor and makes the final dish that bit lighter and crisper. Check out Beer-Battered Beetroot and Cauliflower Bites (page 54) and Hop House 13 Lime Fish Tacos (page 93) to see how well this works.

5. SOUPS AND STEWS

There are certain kinds of soups that come to life with a splash of beer, and Guinness Draught does just that by bringing some bitterness to the sweet onions in Guinness Draught Onion Soup With Irish Cheddar Toast (page 34). Stouts are perfect for stews and braises—after all, Traditional Beef and Guinness Stew (page 72) is a classic for a reason. But don't stop there: Hop House 13 or Baltimore Blonde gives new life to chicken pot pie (Chicken, Leek, and Hop House 13 Pot Pie, page 84), and Foreign Extra Stout enriches Groundnut Chicken and Sweet Potato Stew (page 81). One taste of Beef Cheek, Chorizo, and Foreign Extra Stout Casserole With Mustard Dumplings (page

77) and you'll be a devotee of adding beer to your stew pot.

6. BAKING

Using Guinness in baking doesn't just contribute depth of flavor: The beer helps breads and cakes rise. It prevents the Chocolate, Stout, and Potato Cake (page 109) from being too dense and lightens the Cocoa, Stout, and Fig Loaf (page 125). The dark roasted malts in stouts enhance flavors of coffee and cocoa. Once you've enjoyed the amped-up flavor of stout-rich Guinness Draught Cheesecake Brownies (page 107), you'll never go back to your old brownie recipe. Hop House 13 and Baltimore Blonde each contribute different hoppy aromas that enhance the flavor of both sweet and savory: Enjoy with white chocolate (see White Chocolate and Hop House 13 Cake With Brown Butter Glaze, page 104) or salami and smoked cheese (see Savory Hop House 13 Loaf Cake With Salami and Smoked Scamorza, page 126).

BEER-FRIENDLY INGREDIENTS

STOUTS

Guinness Draft Stout / Extra Stout / Foreign Extra Stout

Black currants, beef, beetroot, black pudding, blue cheese, chocolate, cocoa, coffee, dried fruit, juniper, miso, mushrooms, mustard, oysters, orange, peanut butter, prunes, salmon, smoked fish, treacle, warm spices.

Guinness Over the Moon Milk Stout

Cinnamon, cocoa nibs, dark chocolate, demerara sugar, grilled vegetables, Gouda cheese, mole spices, pecans, roasted lamb, spiced meat, vanilla.

ALE

Baltimore Blonde

Basil, brown butter, carrots, cauliflower, chicken, chives, crab, lemon, mozzarella, Monterey Jack, pesto, salmon, salami, shrimp, smoked cheese, white chocolate.

LAGER

Hop House 13

Apples, berries, chiles, clams, cilantro (coriander), fennel, fresh ginger, goat cheese, lime, milk chocolate, mussels, peaches, ricotta, salami, sausages, tahini, thyme, white fish.

THE
RECIPES

NOTES

- Both US measurements and metric measurements are included in this book. It is important to work with one set of measurements and not alternate between the two within a recipe. For best results, we strongly recommend that all ingredients are weighed on a digital kitchen scale. Cup measurements can vary from cook to cook, while weighing is always accurate. A digital scale is an inexpensive piece of kitchen equipment, and recipe results are more consistent when you use one. It's also a great way of measuring beer!

- Depending on where you live, you might not be able to get ahold of either Hop House 13 or Baltimore Blonde. That's okay! You can use either of these beers in the recipes that call for them. Over the Moon Milk Stout is also only available in certain territories; Foreign Extra Stout can be substituted if this beer isn't available to you.

- When salt is called for, use either fine sea salt or flaky sea salt. We specify which kind in the recipe if it makes a difference. Pepper is always black and freshly ground.

- Butter is either salted or unsalted. If it makes a difference to the recipe, we specify which one to use. All eggs are medium, free range, and for baking, used at room temperature.

- All spoon measures are level. All recipes were tested in a conventional oven. If you're using a fan oven, reduce temperatures by 20 percent.

APPETIZERS & SHAREABLES

COFFEE
AND
FOREIGN EXTRA STOUT PECAN GRANOLA

4 cups (360g) old fashioned rolled oats

1 cup (120g) pecans, coarsely chopped

¼ cup (20g) ground coffee

½ cup (90g) packed light brown sugar

½ teaspoon sea salt

¼ cup (50g) coconut oil

⅓ cup (80ml) Guinness Foreign Extra Stout

¼ cup (85g) maple syrup

Coffee plus Guinness Foreign Extra Stout is an energizing way to start your morning. This granola is not too sweet, with an addictive bitter edge from the beer that will have you sneaking handfuls long after breakfast time is over. Serve with milk or yogurt and fresh berries or sliced bananas. **Yield: 4 cups**

Preheat the oven to 350°F (180°C). Line a large rimmed baking sheet with parchment paper.

In a large bowl, mix together the oats, pecans, coffee, brown sugar, and salt. In a small saucepan over medium heat, warm the coconut oil, stout, and maple syrup for 5 to 6 minutes, until the mixture is smooth and bubbling. Tip the syrup mixture into the oat mixture and stir until everything is well combined.

Spread the granola across the prepared baking sheet and bake for 40 to 45 minutes, stirring every 10 minutes, until golden brown.

Allow the granola to cool on the baking sheet before storing in an airtight jar until ready to serve.

SPICY SCRAMBLED EGGS
WITH
HOP HOUSE 13 FLATBREADS

FLATBREADS

3 cups (360g) self-rising flour

¾ teaspoon sea salt

¾ cup (180ml) Guinness Hop House 13 Lager or Guinness Baltimore Blonde Beer

¾ cup (180ml) plain natural yogurt

1 tablespoon extra-virgin olive oil

Butter for serving

EGGS

2 tablespoons (30g) butter

1 red onion, thinly sliced

1 green chile, seeded and finely chopped

1 teaspoon garam masala

16 cherry tomatoes, halved

8 medium eggs

Ever had one of those mornings when you wake up and there's no bread in the house? These quick Hop House 13 flatbreads will save the day. Serve them with spicy scrambled eggs and enjoy!

Yield: 4 servings

TO MAKE THE FLATBREADS: In a large bowl, mix together the flour and salt. Make a well in the center and add the beer, yogurt, and olive oil. Stir with a wooden spoon until you have a soft dough. Leave the dough to rest for 10 minutes.

Preheat the oven to 300°F (150°C). Cut dough into eight even pieces, weighing each on a kitchen scale to ensure they're equally sized. Flour a work surface. Pat out the pieces on the prepared surface until they are about ½ inch (1.2cm) thick.

Heat a large dry cast-iron skillet over medium-high. When the skillet is hot, place four pieces of dough in the skillet and cook for 5 to 6 minutes on each side, until they are lightly browned and puffed up. Transfer the cooked flatbreads to the oven to keep warm while you make the remaining flatbreads and eggs.

TO MAKE THE EGGS: Wipe out the skillet you used to cook the flatbreads and place over medium heat. Add the butter and melt it. Add the onion and chile and cook for about 5 minutes, until the onion is soft. Add the garam masala, cook for 2 minutes until aromatic, then add the tomatoes. Cook for 2 minutes, then pour in the eggs. Lower the heat to medium-low and stir slowly with your wooden spoon to scramble the eggs until just set, 3 to 4 minutes. Remove from the heat.

Divide the eggs between four warm plates and serve with the flatbreads, split and buttered, on the side.

WELSH RAREBIT

Neither Welsh nor rabbit, Welsh rarebit is basically fancy cheese on toast. Here, Guinness Draught adds a depth of roasted malt flavor that elevates this simple lunch or supper dish. If you're feeling unconventional, add a smear of spicy tomato chutney between bread and cheese for a dash of heat. Purists may howl, but it's always fun to put your own twist on a traditional recipe. **Yield: 2 servings**

2 tablespoons (30g) butter

1 teaspoon Dijon mustard or Chile Extra Stout Mustard (p 62)

2 tablespoons (30ml) Guinness Draught Stout

1 teaspoon Worcestershire sauce

1¾ cups (175g) grated aged cheddar cheese

Four ¾-inch- (2cm-) thick slices sourdough or granary bread

2 tablespoons store-bought or homemade tomato chutney (optional)

1 egg

In a small saucepan over medium heat, gently heat the butter, mustard, stout, and Worcestershire sauce for about 3 to 4 minutes, until the butter melts. Add the cheese and stir to melt, but do not let it boil. You should have a thick paste. Remove from the heat.

Preheat the broiler to medium-high.

Toast the bread lightly on both sides and thickly spread the tomato chutney (if using) on one side of each piece. Whisk the egg into the rarebit mixture and spoon onto the toast. Broil until golden and bubbling. Devour immediately.

HOP HOUSE 13 CHEESE AND SEAWEED SCONES WITH CHIVE BUTTER

These cheese scones are quick to make and perfect if you're in the mood to have a taste of Guinness with your breakfast. Dulse, an edible seaweed, adds an extra layer of salty umami flavor. **Yield: 8 scones**

Preheat the oven to 425°F (220°C). Line a rimmed baking sheet with parchment paper.

TO MAKE THE SCONES: In a large bowl, mix together the flour, ¾ cup (75g) of the cheese, the dulse, and salt. Make a well in the center, add the cream and beer, and stir with a knife until the dough comes together. This is quite a soft mixture. Lightly flour a work surface. Tip the dough onto the prepared surface and pat into a ¾-inch (2cm) thick round.

Transfer the dough to the prepared baking sheet and cut it into eight wedges using a large chef's knife. Separate gently, spacing the scones at least 2 inches (5cm) apart. Brush with milk and sprinkle with the remaining ¼ cup (25g) cheese. Bake for 18 to 22 minutes, until golden. Allow to cool slightly on a wire rack.

TO MAKE THE CHIVE BUTTER: Meanwhile, mix the butter and chives together in a small bowl until well combined. Chill while the scones are cooking. Serve warm scones with slices of cold chive butter.

SCONES

2½ cups (300g) self-rising flour

1 cup (100g) grated mature cheddar cheese, divided

1 tablespoon dulse flakes

¼ teaspoon fine sea salt

⅔ cup (160ml) heavy cream

⅔ cup (160ml) Guinness Hop House 13 Lager or Guinness Baltimore Blonde Beer

Milk for brushing

CHIVE BUTTER

6 tablespoons (90g) salted butter, at room temperature

1 tablespoon finely chopped chives

GUINNESS DRAUGHT ONION SOUP WITH IRISH CHEDDAR TOAST

3 tablespoons (45g) butter

4 onions (about 24 ounces [675g]), thinly sliced

Sea salt

Black pepper

2 tablespoons all-purpose flour

1 teaspoon fresh thyme leaves

1 cup (240ml) Guinness Draught Stout

34 fluid ounces (1L) beef stock

Dash Roe & Co. Blended Irish Whiskey (optional)

4 thick baguette slices

1 tablespoon Dijon mustard or Chile Extra Stout Mustard (page 62)

1 cup (100g) grated Irish cheddar cheese

Sweet, silky caramelized onions and dark malty Guinness goodness are a soup combination made in heaven. Top with melted cheese on bread for full-on comfort. This is a great dish to make in advance, as the flavors improve overnight. **Yield: 4 servings**

Melt the butter in a large heavy-bottom saucepan over medium-low heat. Add the onions, season well with salt and black pepper, and cook, stirring often, for about 1 hour, until the onions are soft, sticky, and deep brown. Stir in the flour and thyme, and cook, stirring, for 3 to 4 minutes.

Whisk in the beer and stock, increase the heat to medium-high, and bring to a boil. Reduce the heat to medium-low and simmer for about 1 hour. Add the whiskey (if using) and season with salt and black pepper as desired.

Heat the broiler to high. Spread the baguette slices with the mustard. Ladle the soup into four ovenproof dishes, top each with a slice of baguette, and sprinkle with the cheese. Broil for 4 to 5 minutes, until the bread is toasted and the cheese is melted and bubbling. Serve immediately.

GRILLED CHEESE + GUINNESS

Here are four types of grilled cheese sandwiches to pair with four types of Guinness. Simply butter the outside of your bread, sandwich the fillings between them, grill, flip, and enjoy! **Yield: 2 servings per recipe**

IRISH TOASTED SPECIAL (WITH GUINNESS HOP HOUSE 13 LAGER)	4 slices white sandwich bread 2 slices ham ¼ onion, thinly sliced	1 cup (100g) grated red cheddar cheese 4 tomato slices
MOZZARELLA, TOMATO, AND PESTO (WITH GUINNESS HOP HOUSE 13 BEER)	2 ciabatta rolls, halved lengthwise 2 tablespoons basil pesto	1 cup (115g) grated mozzarella cheese 4 tomato slices
PROVOLONE, ASPARAGUS, AND CARAMELIZED ONIONS (WITH GUINNESS DRAFT STOUT)	4 slices sourdough bread 4 slices provolone cheese 6 spears asparagus, lightly steamed	2 tablespoons jarred caramelized onions
SWISS CHEESE, HONEY ROAST HAM, AND DIJON MAYO (WITH GUINNESS EXTRA STOUT)	2 onion bagels, halved 4 slices Emmental cheese 2 thick slices honey roast ham	2 tablespoons mayonnaise 2 teaspoons Dijon mustard or Chile Extra Stout Mustard (page 62)

CHEDDAR EXTRA STOUT MUFFINS

Deeply savory from the combination of Extra Stout and cheese, these muffins also take kindly to other additions like crispy bacon bits, chopped ham, olives, or even chopped roasted peppers. Perfect with soup for a wintertime lunch. **Yield: 12 muffins**

2⅓ cups (280g) all-purpose flour

2 teaspoons baking powder

¼ teaspoon sea salt

1 cup (100g) plus ¼ cup (25g) grated mature cheddar cheese

6 tablespoons (90g) butter, melted

½ cup (120ml) plain natural yogurt

½ cup (120ml) Guinness Extra Stout

1 medium egg

Butter for serving

Preheat the oven to 400°F (200°C) and line a 12-cup muffin tin with paper liners.

In a large bowl, sift together the flour, baking powder, and salt, then stir in the cheese. In a small bowl, whisk together the butter, yogurt, stout, and egg. Pour the stout mixture into the flour mixture and gently mix with a wooden spoon until just combined.

Divide the batter between the prepared muffin cups so that they are about two-thirds full, then sprinkle the tops with extra cheese. Bake for 18 to 20 minutes, until the muffins are well risen, golden, and cooked through. Remove from the tin and serve warm with lots of butter.

GUINNESS AND CHEESE:

Which Types of Guinness Pair Well with Which Types of Cheese?

Beer and cheese are the perfect pairing. The carbonation in beer cleanses the palate with each sip, making sure you can taste that cheese to perfection every time. When you're thinking of what cheese to pair with which Guinness, think about balance—you don't want the cheese to overpower the beer or vice versa. Here are a few choice cheeseboard picks for your next at-home happy hour or cocktail party.

Guinness Draught Stout
Well-flavored cheese: mature cheddar, washed rind cheese like Gubbeen

Guinness Extra Stout
Cheese with a little extra: baked Brie with honey and thyme

Guinness Foreign Extra Stout
Full-bodied blues: mature Cashel Blue, Roquefort, Stilton

Guinness Over the Moon Milk Stout
Mild semi-hard cheese: Gouda, mature Edam, cheddar

Guinness Baltimore Blonde Beer
Mild-flavored cheese: young cheddar, Manchego, provolone, mozzarella

Guinness Hop House 13 Lager
Soft creamy cheese: fresh goat cheese, cream cheese, ricotta

CHEDDAR
"toasted mostly" haunted Ben Gunn's dreams on Treasure Island. It has been abused as "mousetrap" and deemed fit for a Queen. Victoria received the largest Cheddar ever made as a wedding present. Cheddar's beauty is that, like Guinness, it is uniformly good wherever it is made.

GUINNESS GUIDE TO ENGLISH CHEESE

STILTON
gives the lie to foreigners who claim the British have no palate. Noblest of our cheeses, it has earned the praise of Lamb and Pope. Indeed, in the last century "prime Stilton" (meaning A 1), was a stock phrase. Authorities say better not to moisten your Stilton with anything; keep your Guinness to drink with it

CHESHIRE
is still what Sir Kenelme Digby called it in the 17th century, "a quick, fat, rich, well tasted cheese." Most people prefer Red Cheshire to White. But everyone agrees that the rare Blue is better than either, and that Guinness is its ideal companion.

WENSLEYDALE
is supposed to have been the invention of the monks of Jervaulx. White Wensleydale is the common variety, with a characteristic fresh taste, but there is a blue variety, now virtually extinct, which many epicures regard as the best of English cheeses.

LEICESTER
is redder than Cheshire, and more crumbly. Distinguished by its mill-stone shape and a flavour said to be even better outdoors than in. Particularly good for making Welsh rabbit or eating with bread, butter and a glass of Guinness.

BLUE VINNY
from Dorset is rare and chalk white with bright blue veins—hence "Blue." The "Vinny" part, however, has nothing to do with veins but derives from a dialect word meaning mould. Eat Blue Vinny with "Dorset Knobs" (hard baked rolls) and Guinness.

LANCASHIRE
is as famous for its cheese as for its lassies. Pale, crumbly and rather strong, Lancashire is technically a hard cheese, in that the original curds are milled, then pressed in a chesset. Lancashire cheese is almost as good with apple pie as with Guinness.

GUINNESS GOES WELL WITH GOOD FOOD
Naturally good in itself, it adds goodness to any good meal

ABOVE: "Guinness Guide to English Cheese" press advertisement, 1940s.

GUINNESS HOP HOUSE 13 GRUYÈRE GOUGÈRES

1 stick (4 ounces [110g]) butter

½ cup (120ml) water

½ cup (120ml) Guinness Hop House 13 Lager or Guinness Baltimore Blonde Beer

½ teaspoon fine sea salt

1¼ cups (150g) all-purpose flour, sifted

5 medium eggs, beaten, divided

1 cup (100g) plus ½ cup (50g) grated Gruyère cheese

1 teaspoon mustard powder

¼ teaspoon cayenne pepper

SPECIAL SUPPLIES
Piping bag and tip (optional)

These bite-size choux pastry puffs, enriched by the addition of beer and Gruyère, are perfect drinks party fare. But be warned! Make plenty or risk running short. They're incredibly moreish, especially when served with a glass of chilled Hop House 13.
Yield: about 30 gougères

Preheat the oven to 425°F (220°C) and line two rimmed baking sheets with parchment paper.

Combine the butter, water, beer, and salt in a medium saucepan over medium heat, stirring until the butter melts. Bring the mixture to a boil, then remove the pan from the heat and add the flour. Mix thoroughly with a wooden spoon (it will look rather like mashed potatoes), then place the pan over low heat. Cook, stirring, for 2 to 3 minutes, until the mixture forms a smooth ball.

Remove the pan from the heat and allow the dough to cool slightly for about 5 minutes. One at a time, beat in four of the eggs, until the mixture is smooth and glossy. Stir in 1 cup (100g) cheese, the mustard powder, and cayenne pepper.

If piping your pastry, transfer the dough to a piping bag fitted with a ½-inch (1.2cm) plain tip. Pipe teaspoonfuls of the choux pastry on to the prepared baking sheets (alternatively, use a teaspoon to scoop and drop the dough). Make sure to leave 1 inch (2.5cm) between each pastry.

Glaze the pastry by brushing each with the remaining egg and sprinkle with remaining ½ cup (50g) cheese. Put them into the oven and immediately turn the temperature down to 375°F (190°C). Bake for 20 to 25 minutes, until the pastry is golden, crisp, and light. Devour while still warm.

SPICED HOP HOUSE 13 AND POMEGRANATE MOLASSES- ROASTED CHICKPEAS

One 14-ounce (400g) can chickpeas, drained and rinsed

2 tablespoons Guinness Hop House 13 Lager or Guinness Baltimore Blonde Beer

2 teaspoons sriracha

2 teaspoons pomegranate molasses

1 tablespoon extra-virgin olive oil

Flaky sea salt

Snacks to go with beer are always better if they include beer in the ingredients. Hop House 13 brings a hoppy note to the heat-sweet-salt triumvirate, making these vegan-friendly chickpeas absolutely irresistible.
Yield: 2 to 4 servings

Preheat the oven to 400°F (200°C). Place the chickpeas in a large bowl. In a small bowl or glass measuring cup, whisk together the beer, sriracha, pomegranate molasses, and olive oil.

Pour the beer mixture over the chickpeas, tossing to mix well. Spread the chickpeas on a rimmed baking sheet in a single layer. Season well with salt.

Bake for 20 to 25 minutes, stirring every 10 minutes, until the chickpeas are crunchy. Eat while warm.

HOP HOUSE 13 PIZZA WITH BLACK PUDDING, BLUE CHEESE, AND APPLE

This super-fast tomato sauce works well with the extra hoppy flavor that the pizza base gets from the Hop House 13. **Yield: 2 large pizzas**

DOUGH

4 cups (480g) strong white bread flour

1 tablespoon granulated sugar

½ teaspoon sea salt

One ¼-ounce (7g) packet instant dry yeast

One 11.2-fluid-ounce (330ml) bottle Guinness Hop House 13 Lager or Guinness Baltimore Blonde Beer

2 tablespoons extra-virgin olive oil, plus more for oiling dough

Semolina or cornmeal for dusting

SAUCE

One 14-ounce (400g) can plum tomatoes

1 tablespoon balsamic vinegar

1 tablespoon extra-virgin olive oil

½ teaspoon dried oregano

Sea salt

Black pepper

TOPPING

6 ounces (170g) black pudding, sliced into ½-inch (1.2cm) rounds

5 ounces (140g) Cashel Blue or similar creamy blue cheese, crumbled

1 crisp apple, cored and thinly sliced

Extra-virgin olive oil for drizzling

Black pepper

Place the flour in a large bowl. Add the sugar, salt, and yeast, and stir to combine. Make a well in the center of the flour mixture, pour in the beer and olive oil, and mix together well until a dough comes together. Allow the dough to sit for 5 minutes.

Lightly dust a work surface with flour. Turn the dough out on the surface and knead for about 10 minutes, until smooth and springy. Add a little olive oil to the bowl and turn the dough around in the bowl to coat, making sure the entire ball is well oiled. Cover with a tea towel and leave in a warm place for about 1 hour, until the dough has doubled in size.

Divide the dough in half, then roll each half into a ball. Cover and let rest for at least 15 minutes.

While the dough rests, make the tomato sauce. In a deep bowl, combine the tomatoes, vinegar, olive oil, and oregano. Blend with an immersion blender until smooth and season with salt and black pepper.

Preheat the oven to 500°F (260°C).

Dust a work surface with semolina and, working with one ball at a time, push and stretch the dough until it's about 12 inches (30cm) in diameter and as thin as possible. Repeat with the second ball. You should now have two raw pizza crusts. Sprinkle two large rimmed baking sheets with semolina and slide the uncooked crusts onto them.

Top each crust with the tomato sauce, black pudding, blue cheese, and apple. Drizzle with olive oil and sprinkle with black pepper.

Bake each pizza for 12 to 15 minutes, until golden and crispy. Serve.

CAMPFIRE COOKOUT BEER-SIMMERED SAUSAGES

8 large meaty sausages

One 11.2-fluid-ounce (330ml) bottle Guinness Hop House 13 Lager or Guinness Baltimore Blonde Beer

8 small hot dog rolls

Mustard, ketchup, and/or gherkins for serving

Summertime cookouts are never complete without sausages and beer. Guinness Hop House 13 adds a sweet biscuity malt flavor to the sausages, and because they're cooked when you put them over the fire, they're ready before anyone gets too hungry. And with the remaining heat of the fire, you can cook s'mores!

Yield: 4 servings

Place the sausages in a large saucepan and pour in the beer. Add some water if there's not enough beer to cover the sausages. Bring the pan to a simmer over medium heat and poach for 5 to 6 minutes, until just cooked. Drain the sausages in a colander.

Meanwhile, light a campfire or charcoal grill. Gather long sticks to use as skewers, making sure to avoid toxic trees or shrubs, and carve or break a point on the end. As soon as the flames die down, leaving white coals, push a sausage lengthwise onto the stick and hold it over the fire.

Cook until the sausages are crisp and nicely browned, then slide them onto the hot dog rolls and add mustard, ketchup, and gherkins as desired. Enjoy immediately!

TIP Cooking sausages over an open fire using foraged sticks and branches is an incredibly fun summertime activity, but do have caution regarding what kind of wood you gather. Be sure you're thoroughly familiar with the greenery in your area to know which plants and trees to avoid. Consult a local guidebook or park website before beginning your foraging, and if you have any doubts about a plant, leave it and move on to another.

ON THE SIDE:
SIDE DISHES, SALADS & SAUCES

STOUT, PEANUT, AND MISO NOODLE SALAD

The Guinness Draught gives a lovely depth of flavor to these noodles, with the bitterness of the beer playing nicely with the salty miso. If you feel like adding more protein, toss in some shredded cooked chicken or cooked prawns before serving. **Yield: 4 servings**

Cook the noodles according to the package instructions, adding peas for the last 2 minutes of cooking. Drain and rinse thoroughly under cold water. Set aside until completely cooled.

In a large bowl, whisk together the peanut butter and beer to loosen, then mix in the miso, sesame oil, soy sauce, and lime juice to make a smooth dressing. Add the noodles and peas along with the scallions, chile, and cilantro, tossing to coat. Season with black pepper.

Serve with the sesame seeds on top and lime wedges on the side.

9 ounces (250g) thin dried egg noodles

6 ounces (170g) frozen peas

5 tablespoons (75g) crunchy peanut butter

2 tablespoons Guinness Draught Stout

1 teaspoon miso

2 tablespoons toasted sesame oil

1 tablespoon soy sauce

Juice of 2 limes

4 scallions, both white and green parts, sliced at an angle

1 red chile, sliced

1 small bunch fresh cilantro (coriander), chopped

Black pepper

2 tablespoons sesame seeds, toasted

Lime wedges for serving

BEER-BATTERED BEETROOT AND CAULIFLOWER BITES

A perfect game-day snack, this fried beetroot and cauliflower dish just happens to be vegan. Guinness Draught adds color to the batter, but more important, it also contributes a malty sweetness that enhances the flavor of the vegetables. **Yield: 4 servings**

1 small cauliflower (about 1 pound [450g]), trimmed and broken into bite-size florets

2 beetroots (about 9 ounces [250g]), trimmed and unpeeled

Vegetable oil for deep frying

1¾ cups (210g) self-rising flour

½ teaspoon fine sea salt

One 11.2-fluid-ounce (330ml) bottle Guinness Draught Stout, very cold

Flaky sea salt for serving

Lemon wedges for serving

In a large saucepan over medium-high heat, bring about 1 inch (2.5cm) of water to a boil. Place the cauliflower in a steaming basket or heatproof colander and carefully place it over the boiling water. Cover and steam for 2 minutes. Remove the cauliflower and allow to cool.

Meanwhile, put the beetroots in a medium saucepan and add cold water to cover. Bring to a boil over medium-high heat, then turn the heat to medium-low. Simmer for 30 to 40 minutes, until the beetroots are tender. Drain and allow to cool. Rub off the skins and cut into ½-inch (1.2cm) rounds.

Heat 2 inches (5cm) of vegetable oil in a deep fryer or deep saucepan fitted with a fry thermometer to 365°F (185°C). In a large bowl, mix together the flour and salt. Add the beer and whisk to make a smooth batter.

Dip the beetroot rounds and cauliflower florets into the batter, shaking off the excess. Using metal tongs, carefully lower the battered pieces into the oil. Cook in batches for 3 to 4 minutes, until crisp and golden, then use a metal slotted spoon to quickly transfer the bites to kitchen towels to drain.

Sprinkle with the flaky salt and serve with lemon wedges.

HOP HOUSE 13 GLAZED CARROTS

Glazed carrots are a classic dish to accompany the Sunday roast; the addition of Guinness Hop House 13 adds a lovely hit of bitterness that accentuates the sweetness of the carrots. **Yield: 4 servings**

4 carrots (about 18 ounces [500g]), peeled and cut into ¾-inch (2cm) diagonal slices

2 tablespoons (30g) butter

¼ teaspoon sea salt

¾ cup (180ml) Guinness Hop House 13 Lager or Guinness Baltimore Blonde Beer

2 tablespoons chopped fresh flat-leaf parsley or lovage

Place the carrots in a wide, shallow pan over medium heat. Add the butter, salt, and beer. Cover and simmer for 10 minutes, until the carrots start to soften.

Remove the lid from the pan and continue to cook for another 10 to 12 minutes, stirring occasionally, until the liquid has reduced to glaze the carrots. Sprinkle with the parsley and serve.

CARAMELIZED ONION, EXTRA STOUT, AND BLUE CHEESE TART

2 tablespoons (30g) butter

2 to 3 large red onions (about 18 ounces [500g]), halved and thinly sliced

1 tablespoon light brown sugar

½ teaspoon sea salt

⅓ cup (80ml) Guinness Extra Stout

One 12-ounce (340g) sheet ready-rolled puff pastry, all-butter if possible

2 tablespoons Dijon mustard or Chile Extra Stout Mustard (page 62)

4 ounces (110g) Cashel Blue or similar creamy blue cheese, crumbled

1 tablespoon fresh thyme leaves

1 egg, beaten

Sweet caramelized onions get a deliciously bitter counterpoint from Guinness Extra Stout and make a tasty base for your favorite blue cheese. Perfect for lunch or a light supper. **Yield: 4 servings**

In a wide shallow pan over medium heat, melt the butter. Add the onions, brown sugar, and salt. Stir well and cover with a lid. Cook for about 10 minutes, until the onions are wilted, then remove the lid and add the stout. Cook for 30 minutes, stirring often, until the onions are golden and the liquid has evaporated.

Preheat the oven to 425°F (220°C). Line a rimmed baking sheet with parchment paper.

Unroll the pastry onto the prepared baking sheet. Using a sharp knife, score a ¾-inch (2cm) border around the edge of the pastry, but don't cut all the way through. Spread the mustard inside the border and scatter the onion mixture on top. Top with the blue cheese and thyme. Brush the edge of the pastry with the egg.

Bake for 18 to 20 minutes, until the pastry is puffed and golden brown. Serve.

HOP HOUSE 13 BOULANGÈRE POTATOES

Delicious with a roast dinner, these potatoes must be cut carefully, as their thickness makes all the difference when it comes to the cooking time. Ideally, use a mandoline or food processor to slice them thinly, or else sharpen your knife and carefully slice as thin as you can. **Yield: 8 servings**

4 tablespoons (60g) butter, divided, plus more for greasing dish

2 onions, halved and thinly sliced

3⅓ pounds (1.5kg) floury potatoes, such as Maris Piper or Yukon Gold, peeled and cut into ¼-inch (6mm) slices

Sea salt

Black pepper

1½ cups (360ml) vegetable stock

½ cup (120ml) Guinness Hop House 13 Lager or Guinness Baltimore Blonde Beer

Preheat the oven to 350°F (180°C). With a bit of butter, grease an 8-by-12-inch (20-by-30cm) baking dish.

In a large sauté pan or skillet over medium heat, melt 2 tablespoons (30g) of the butter. Add the onions and cook for 8 to 10 minutes, until they are soft and golden.

Spread one-third of the potatoes over the base of the prepared baking dish. Cover with half of the onions, then season with salt and pepper. Continue layering potatoes and onions, seasoning each layer, and finishing with a top layer of potatoes.

Season the top layer with salt and black pepper, dot with the remaining 2 tablespoons (30g) butter, and pour in the stock and beer.

Bake for 50 to 60 minutes, until the potatoes are tender and the top is crisp and golden. Serve.

HASSELBACK POTATOES WITH HOP HOUSE 13 AND CHIVE SAUCE

Potatoes and beer—what could be more Irish? In this recipe, this classic combination has been re-imagined in a new delicious way. Hasselback potatoes always look impressive, and when you serve them with this creamy Hop House 13 and chive sauce, they make the perfect side for bacon or ham. **Yield: 6 servings**

POTATOES

2¼ pounds (1kg) baby potatoes, scrubbed

2 tablespoons extra-virgin olive oil

1 tablespoon finely chopped fresh rosemary

Flaky sea salt

Black pepper

SAUCE

½ cup (120ml) milk

One 8-ounce (225g) package cream cheese

¼ teaspoon sea salt

½ teaspoon black pepper

¼ cup (60ml) Guinness Hop House 13 Lager or Guinness Baltimore Blonde Beer

1 cup (50g) chopped chives

Preheat the oven to 400°F (200°C).

TO MAKE THE POTATOES: Place the potatoes, one at a time, into the bowl of a wooden spoon lying flat on your work surface and, using a sharp knife, make small vertical slits at ⅓-inch (1cm) intervals all along its length. The spoon will stop the knife from slicing all the way through the potato.

Transfer the potatoes to a large rimmed baking sheet. In a small bowl, mix together the olive oil and rosemary. Use a pastry brush to coat the potatoes with the rosemary oil, working it into the gaps between the slices. Season with the flaky salt and pepper to taste.

Roast, brushing the potatoes occasionally with the rosemary oil from the pan, for 45 minutes to 1 hour, until they are golden, crispy, and cooked through.

TO MAKE THE SAUCE: Meanwhile, in a heavy-bottom saucepan over low heat, whisk together the milk, cream cheese, salt, and pepper until combined. Add the beer and stir until smooth. Remove from the heat and mix in the chives.

Serve the sauce in a sauce boat alongside the potatoes.

ENTRÉES

OPEN GATE BREWERY 1817 BURGER

One 8-ounce (225g) chuck, short rib, or brisket burger patty

Sea salt

Black pepper

2 thick Irish cheddar cheese slices (e.g., Dubliner or similar brand)

3 tablespoons (45g) Beer-Braised Onions (recipe follows)

1 tablespoon (15g) butter, melted

1 brioche bun

2 beefsteak tomato slices

2 tablespoons Bacon and Roasted Garlic Aioli (recipe follows)

2 Bibb lettuce leaves, washed well

2 cooked thick-cut applewood smoked bacon slices

Taking its name from the year the first shipment of Guinness was sent from Ireland to the United States, this burger is the number one selling item at the Open Gate Brewery in Baltimore. According to chef Kevin McCarthy, "It has been popular since the day we opened. It's where Dublin meets an American classic: layers of beef patty, Irish cheddar cheese, bacon, Hop House 13–braised onions, and bacon aioli." You heard that right. Bacon aioli. Come for the burger, stay for the irresistible bacon aioli.

Yield: 1 burger

Season the burger patty with salt and pepper. Heat a cast-iron skillet over medium-high heat. When the pan is hot, add the patty and cook, flipping once, to the desired doneness, about 3 to 5 minutes per side. After you've flipped the patty, add the cheese on top to melt, followed by the onions.

Smear the butter on both sides of the bun and toast. Season the tomato slices with salt and black pepper.

To build the burger, spread the aioli on the bottom bun, then top with the lettuce leaves, tomato slices, and cooked bacon slices. Place the burger patty on top, then top with the other side of the bun and enjoy.

BEER-BRAISED ONIONS

1 tablespoon vegetable oil	Black pepper
1 tablespoon (15g) butter	2 onions, cut into ¼-inch (6mm) slices
1 tablespoon brown sugar	
Sea salt	2 tablespoons Guinness Hop House 13 Beer

In a large nonstick pan over medium-high heat, heat the vegetable oil and butter together until the butter melts. Stir in the brown sugar, then season with salt and black pepper. Add the onions and cook, stirring often, for 6 to 8 minutes, until onions are beginning to turn translucent.

Turn the heat down to medium-low. Cook the onions for 45 minutes, stirring occasionally, until they are fully cooked and caramel in color and the liquid is absorbed. Remove the pan from the heat and stir in the beer, one tablespoon at a time.

Place the pan back over low heat until the liquid is reduced, no more than five minutes. Use right away or store in an airtight container in the fridge for three to five days.

(CONTINUED ON PAGE 68)

BACON AND ROASTED GARLIC AIOLI

6 garlic cloves, left whole and peeled

1 cup (240ml) extra-virgin olive oil

4 thick-cut applewood smoked bacon slices, cut into ¼ in. (½ cm) cubes

3 medium egg yolks

1 tablespoon lemon juice

1 teaspoon white vinegar

Preheat the oven to 350°F.

Place the garlic cloves in a small oven-safe dish and cover with enough of the olive oil to submerge them completely (reserve the rest of the oil in a measuring cup). Cover the dish with aluminum foil and roast for about 30 minutes, or until the cloves have softened. Strain the garlic oil back into the reserved oil, reserving the roasted garlic. Set the oil and roasted garlic aside.

Set a large sauté pan or skillet over medium-low heat and place the bacon in the pan. Cook for 5 to 8 minutes, until the bacon fat is rendered and the bacon is cooked but not crisp. Strain the bacon fat into the oil, reserving the bacon bits. You should have about 1 cup (240ml) of fat and oil. If it is short, top up with plain olive oil.

In the bowl of a food processor, combine the egg yolks and roasted garlic. While the machine runs, very slowly drizzle in the oil until it has all been incorporated. Add the lemon juice and vinegar, and pulse to combine. If the aioli is too thick, add one to two teaspoons of water until it reaches your preferred consistency. Fold in the bacon bits and enjoy. Store in an airtight container in the fridge for up to two weeks.

PORK CHOPS IN GUINNESS DRAUGHT AND BLACK CURRANT SAUCE

Guinness Draught and black currant is a classic Irish pub combination, stemming from the addition of black currant cordial to a pint of Guinness for those who like some sweetness in their glass. The roast character of Guinness Draught and tart, tangy sweetness of black currant makes an even better combination in a sauce to accompany pork chops. Serve this with creamy mashed potatoes and steamed green vegetables. **Yield: 4 servings**

Heat a large heavy-bottom skillet over high heat until hot. Rub the pork chops with vegetable oil, then season with salt and black pepper. Place the chops in the pan and cook one side for about 4 to 5 minutes, until browned and easily released from the pan. Turn and cook the other side for about 2 to 3 minutes, until browned. Continue to cook each side for about 5 minutes, or until the meat has reached an internal temperature of 145°F (62°C). Transfer the chops to a warm plate, cover, and allow to rest.

Meanwhile, pour off the excess fat from the skillet and place it over medium heat. Add the beer to deglaze the pan, whisking while it bubbles. Add the cordial, mustard, and sage, then the butter, whisking all the time, until the sauce reduces, turns glossy, and thickens a little, 4 to 5 minutes. Season with salt and black pepper.

Nestle the chops, and any juices that have collected on the plate, into the sauce, bring back to a simmer, then serve immediately.

4 pork chops, skin and fat scored

Vegetable oil

Sea salt

Black pepper

½ cup (125ml) Guinness Draught Stout

2 tablespoons black currant cordial

1 teaspoon Dijon mustard

1 teaspoon chopped fresh sage

1 tablespoon (15g) butter, fridge cold

HOP HOUSE 13 TOAD IN THE HOLE WITH ONION GRAVY

TOAD

1¼ cups (150g) all-purpose flour

3 medium eggs, beaten

⅓ cup (80ml) milk

One 11.2-fluid-ounce (330ml) bottle Guinness Hop House 13 Lager or Guinness Baltimore Blonde Beer

1 tablespoon whole grain mustard

Pinch sea salt

3 tablespoons beef drippings or extra-virgin olive oil

8 plain pork sausages

GRAVY

1 tablespoon (15g) butter

1 onion, thinly sliced

1 teaspoon light brown sugar

1 tablespoon all-purpose flour

2 cups (480ml) chicken or vegetable stock

Sea salt

Black pepper

Sausages in batter—can it get any better? Add a bottle of Hop House 13 and you're on to a winner, with the beer giving the batter a helping of hop flavor and more of a rise in the oven. Make this into a veggie main course by subbing in meatless sausages and vegetable stock. Try serving this with a bowl of buttered broccoli on the side. **Yield: 4 servings**

Preheat the oven to 425°F (220°C).

TO MAKE THE TOAD: Sift the flour into a large bowl and make a well in the center. Pour in the eggs and whisk together, gradually adding the milk and beer, until the batter is smooth and the consistency of heavy cream. Stir in the mustard and salt. Allow to sit for at least 15 minutes.

Meanwhile, add the drippings and sausages to an 8-by-12-inch (20-by-30cm) roasting pan. Roast for 10 minutes, until the sausages are sizzling and browned.

Remove from the oven and, as quickly as possible, pour the batter around the sausages. Immediately return the pan to the oven and bake for 30 to 35 minutes, until browned and well risen.

TO MAKE THE GRAVY: Meanwhile, in a large sauté pan or skillet over medium heat, melt the butter. Add the onion and cook for about 20 minutes, until the onion is soft and golden. Add the brown sugar, cook for 2 minutes, then sprinkle on the flour. Cook, stirring, for 2 to 3 minutes, then gradually pour in the stock, stirring well. Simmer for 10 minutes, until thickened, then season well with salt and black pepper.

Serve the toad with the gravy.

TRADITIONAL BEEF AND GUINNESS STEW

Many cultures have a variation on beef stew, always made with ingredients on hand. The French use Burgundy wine to make beef bourguignon. In Hungary, paprika is introduced to the pot for goulash. Belgium has carbonnade à la flamande made with Belgian ale. And Ireland has beef and Guinness stew, a hearty and wholesome dish that will keep you warm and comfortable no matter what the weather throws at you. This stew is a popular pub lunch, and you can travel the country trying different variations at every bar you visit. With meat, veg, potatoes, and Guinness, this is the very definition of a meal in a bowl. **Yield: 4 to 6 servings**

2 tablespoons beef drippings or extra-virgin olive oil

2 pounds (900g) stewing steak, cut into 1-inch (2.5cm) pieces

2 onions, sliced

2 celery stalks, finely chopped

3 carrots, peeled and cut into 2-inch (5cm) chunks

2 tablespoons all-purpose flour

One 14.9-fluid-ounce (440ml) can Guinness Draught Stout

1 cup (240ml) beef stock

1 tablespoon apple jelly or red currant jelly

2 tablespoons tomato paste

1 teaspoon Dijon mustard or Chile Extra Stout Mustard (page 62)

2 sprigs fresh thyme

2 bay leaves

Sea salt

Black pepper

8 ounces (225g) baby potatoes, scrubbed

In a heavy-bottom lidded ovenproof casserole dish or Dutch oven over medium-high heat, heat the drippings. Add the meat in batches and cook for about 10 minutes, or until lightly browned, scooping each batch onto a plate as it is done.

If the pan is too dry, add a little more fat as needed, then add the onions, celery, and carrots. Cook for 5 minutes, until the vegetables are starting to soften. Sprinkle with the flour and cook, stirring often, for 2 to 3 minutes. Add the beer, stock, jelly, tomato paste, and mustard, and bring to a boil, stirring and scraping to dissolve all the browned bits on the bottom of the pan. Return the meat to the pan, along with the thyme and bay leaves. Season with salt and black pepper, and cover with the lid. Turn the heat to low and simmer very gently for 2 hours.

Add the potatoes and continue to simmer for 1 hour more, until the potatoes and meat are tender. Season with salt and black pepper, remove and discard the bay leaves and thyme stems, and serve.

TIP This stew can also be cooked in the oven at 325°F (160°C) for 2 hours before adding the potatoes. After you add the potatoes, continue to cook for 1 hour more, until everything is tender.

DUBLIN GUINNESS STOREHOUSE BRAISED BEEF SHORT RIB WITH FOREIGN EXTRA STOUT JUS, DUCK FAT ROASTED POTATOES, AND CELERIAC PURÉE

An extremely popular dish at the Guinness Storehouse in Dublin, this short rib recipe from Head Chef Sean Hunter is a true showstopper. Chef Hunter likes using Foreign Extra Stout here, as it has more pronounced flavors than Guinness Draught, adding roasted, bitter, sweet, rich umami notes to the dish. Serve with Duck Fat Roasted Potatoes and Celeriac Purée for a hearty, yet elevated, dining experience. **Yield: 4 servings**

Sea salt

Black pepper

One 4.5 lb (2 kg) beef short rib on the bone (also known as Jacob's Ladder)

¼ cup (60ml) Irish rapeseed oil

2 large onions, roughly chopped

2 carrots, peeled and chopped

1 bunch celery, chopped

6 garlic cloves, left whole and peeled

4 bay leaves

6 sprigs fresh thyme, divided

6 sprigs fresh rosemary, divided

3 tablespoons tomato purée

34 fluid ounces (1L) plus 1 cup (240ml) Guinness Draught Stout, divided

34 fluid ounces (1L) beef stock

2 shallots, sliced

Cornflour for thickening jus (optional)

Duck Fat Roasted Potatoes for serving (recipe follows)

Celeriac Purée for serving (recipe follows)

Preheat the oven to 375°F (190°C).

Rub salt and black pepper all over the short rib, ensuring it is well coated. Heat a large sauté pan or skillet over medium-high heat. When the pan is hot, add the short rib and sear on all sides until browned, about 3 minutes per side. Remove the short rib from the pan and set it aside.

Place the same pan over medium heat and add the Irish rapeseed oil. Add the onions, carrots, celery, garlic, bay leaves, and half of the thyme and rosemary, and cook until the vegetables are soft, about 10 minutes. Add the tomato purée and 34 ounces (1L) of the stout, and cook for about 10 to 15 minutes, or until liquid is reduced by half. Add the stock, bring to a boil, and pour everything into a large ovenproof casserole dish.

Nestle the short rib among the veggies, making sure it's 90 percent submerged in the liquid (add additional water to the dish if necessary to achieve this). Place the remaining half of thyme and rosemary on top. Cut a piece of parchment paper to the same size and shape as the casserole dish, and tuck it around the meat and vegetables so the parchment paper sits inside the dish. Then cover the dish with aluminium foil.

Braise for 4 hours, until until the internal temperature has reached 320°F (160°C) and beef is very soft and falling off the bone.

Carefully remove the short rib from the braising liquid and transfer it to a rimmed baking sheet to cool slightly. Turn the oven up to 400°F (200°C).

Portion the rib by cutting alongside the thick bones. You can remove the meat entirely from the bone, but leaving the bone in makes for a more attractive presentation when serving. Return the portioned rib to the oven on the rimmed baking sheet and cook for another 15 minutes.

Strain the braising liquid through a sieve, reserving the liquid. Discard the vegetables.

POT ROAST CAULIFLOWER WITH HARISSA-BEER BUTTER

Giving cauliflower the pot roast treatment is a lovely way of making this gorgeous vegetable the star of the table. Hop House 13 brings a delicious citrus note that enhances the flavor of the harissa-beer butter. Serve with a simple tomato sauce and coconut rice.

Yield: 4 to 6 servings

1 large head cauliflower (about 2¼ pounds [1kg])

1 cup (240ml) Guinness Hop House 13 Lager or Guinness Baltimore Blonde Beer

3 garlic cloves, thinly sliced

4 tablespoons (60g) butter, cubed

1 tablespoon harissa

Sea salt

Black pepper

Juice of ½ lime

2 tablespoons toasted flaked almonds

Preheat the oven to 400°F (200°C).

Level the base and trim the leaves from the cauliflower. Bring a large saucepan of salted water to a boil over high heat. Lower the cauliflower into the boiling water, then turn the heat down to low and simmer for 15 minutes. Drain and leave the cauliflower to steam dry in a colander for 5 minutes.

Combine the beer and garlic in a small, deep saucepan over medium heat and bring to a simmer. Simmer for about 10 minutes, until the mixture is reduced by half (beware of the beer bubbling up because of the carbonation). Whisk in the butter, one cube at a time, until the mixture thickens. Stir in the harissa.

Place the cauliflower, stem-side down, in a large, deep ovenproof dish or Dutch oven. Pour the harissa-beer butter over the cauliflower and season with salt and black pepper. Roast for 25 to 30 minutes, basting occasionally, until the cauliflower is tender and well browned.

Carefully transfer the cauliflower to a serving dish. Drizzle lime juice over it, sprinkle with the almonds, and serve.

GROUNDNUT CHICKEN AND SWEET POTATO STEW WITH FOREIGN EXTRA STOUT

First brewed in 1801 (as West Indies Porter), Guinness Foreign Extra Stout was designed for export with extra hops and alcohol to help it withstand long journeys by ship. It's been such a favorite in Africa that Guinness's first overseas brewery outside Ireland and the UK opened in Nigeria in 1963. Nigeria is also one of the world's largest producers of groundnuts, or peanuts, and this groundnut stew, with a touch of extra flavor from Foreign Extra Stout, is an homage to the beer's popularity in Africa. Serve with steamed rice or couscous. **Yield: 4 servings**

2¼ pounds (1kg) bone-in skinless chicken thighs

½ teaspoon fine sea salt

1 teaspoon black pepper

2 tablespoons vegetable oil, divided

1 large onion, sliced

1 inch (2.5cm) fresh ginger, peeled and grated

2 garlic cloves, thinly sliced

3 tablespoons tomato paste

½ cup (120g) crunchy peanut butter

2 cups (480ml) chicken stock

¾ cup (180ml) Guinness Foreign Extra Stout

1 Scotch bonnet chile

3 to 4 small sweet potatoes (14 ounces [400g]) sweet potatoes, peeled and cut into ½-inch (1.2cm) pieces (about 3½ cups)

Chopped roasted peanuts for serving

Chopped fresh cilantro (coriander) for serving

Lime wedges for serving

Season the chicken with the salt and black pepper. In a large skillet over medium heat, heat 1 tablespoon of the vegetable oil until it shimmers. Add the chicken and brown on all sides, 10 to 12 minutes. Remove chicken from the pan and set aside. Remove excess oil from pan.

Heat the remaining 1 tablespoon oil in the same pan over medium heat. Add the onion and cook for 8 to 10 minutes, until soft and brown. Add the ginger, garlic, and tomato paste. Cook, stirring, for 5 minutes, then whisk in the peanut butter, stock, and stout.

Return the chicken to the pan and turn the heat to low. Pierce the chile with a knife (so that it contributes flavor rather than heat) and add it and the sweet potatoes to the pan. Cover and cook for about 25 minutes, until the chicken is cooked through, or until a meat thermometer reads 165°F (75°C), sweet potatoes are tender, and the sauce has reduced slightly.

Remove and discard the chile (unless you want the heat). Sprinkle the stew with peanuts and cilantro, and serve with lime wedges.

STICKY, SPICY BEER CAN CHICKEN

It's a simple idea that has a great payoff: Grill a chicken vertically on top of an open beer can for tender, juicy, flavorsome results. Just make sure you remove the widget in the can before you start cooking! **Yield: 4 to 6 servings**

2 tablespoons extra-virgin olive oil

1 tablespoon smoked paprika

1 teaspoon dried thyme leaves

1 teaspoon black pepper

1 teaspoon ground cumin

½ teaspoon ground coriander

½ teaspoon sea salt

¼ teaspoon cayenne pepper, plus more as desired

One 14.9-fluid-ounce (440ml) can Guinness Draught

One 3½-pound (1.5kg) whole chicken

2 tablespoons barbecue sauce or Guinness Foreign Extra Stout Barbecue Sauce (page 63)

Preheat a lidded grill, bringing the temperature to between 350° and 375°F (180° and 190°C).

Make a rub by mixing together the olive oil, paprika, thyme, black pepper, cumin, coriander, salt, and cayenne pepper in a small bowl.

Open the can of beer and pour half into a glass (to drink!). Using a can opener, remove the top of the can and fish out the widget. Add 1 teaspoon of rub to the can and stir. Massage the remaining rub all over the chicken, inside and out.

Carefully set the chicken, legs down, onto the can so that it fits into the cavity and the chicken looks like it is sitting upright.

Place the chicken upright on the grill, close the lid, and roast for 1½ hours, or until the internal temperature reaches 165°F (75°C). Carefully brush the chicken with the barbecue sauce and continue to cook with the lid down for another 10 minutes.

Carefully remove the chicken from the grill—the can and beer will be extremely hot—and allow to rest for 15 minutes before removing the can, carving the chicken, and serving.

TIP This chicken can also be roasted in the oven. Preheat the oven to 400°F (200°C). Place the chicken upright on the can in a roasting pan. Pour the extra half can of beer into the base of the tray—add 2¼ pounds (1kg) small waxy potatoes (tossed in a little olive oil) if desired—then roast for 1 hour 20 minutes, or until the chicken is golden brown and reaches an internal temperature of 165°F (75°C). Brush with barbecue sauce, cook for another 10 minutes, and allow to rest for 15 minutes before removing the can, carving the chicken, and serving.

CHICKEN, LEEK, AND HOP HOUSE 13 POT PIE

Chicken and Guinness Draught have been friends for a long time; now it's Hop House 13's turn to get in on the act. Citrus notes in the beer brighten up the sauce, making this simple dish one to remember. It's also a good one to make with any leftovers from your Sticky, Spicy Beer Can Chicken (see page 82). If you have the Middle Eastern spice blend za'atar on hand, sprinkle it on the pastry before baking. The herbal flavors work perfectly with this sauce. Serve with a bowl of buttered peas. **Yield: 4 servings**

3 tablespoons (45g) butter

2 leeks, washed well, trimmed, and sliced crosswise into 1 inch (2.5cm) rounds

4 boneless skinless chicken breasts, cut into bite-size pieces, or about 4 cups (550g) cooked chicken

1 garlic clove, minced

⅓ cup (40g) all-purpose flour

One 11.2-fluid-ounce (330ml) bottle Guinness Hop House 13 Lager or Guinness Baltimore Blonde Beer

¾ cup (180ml) milk

Sea salt

Black pepper

One 12-ounce (340g) sheet ready-rolled butter puff pastry

1 egg, beaten

1 tablespoon za'atar (optional)

In a large sauté pan or skillet over medium heat, melt the butter. Add the leeks and cook for about 10 minutes, until they are softened. Add the chicken and cook, stirring, for 4 to 5 minutes. Add the garlic and flour and cook, stirring, for 2 minutes.

Slowly add the beer and milk, stirring all the time. Bring to a boil, then turn the heat to medium-low and simmer for 5 to 6 minutes, until the filling has thickened. Season with salt and black pepper, then spoon the filling into a 2½-quart (2.5L) pie dish. Set aside to cool.

Preheat the oven to 425°F (220°C). Unroll the pastry and cut out a piece slightly larger than the dish. Drape the pastry over the filling and press down the edges. Brush with the egg and, using a sharp knife, make two or three slits in the pastry. Sprinkle with the za'atar (if using).

Place the pie on a rimmed baking sheet, in case it drips, and bake for 40 to 45 minutes, until the filling is bubbling and the pastry is golden brown. Let the pie sit for 10 minutes before serving.

HOP HOUSE 13-POACHED SHRIMP AND PASTA

7 ounces (200g) spaghetti

2 tablespoons (30g) salted butter, divided

2 garlic cloves, thinly sliced

½ fresh red chile, seeded and finely chopped

⅓ cup plus 1 tablespoon (95ml) Guinness Hop House 13 Lager or Guinness Baltimore Blonde Beer

14 ounces (400g) raw shrimp, peeled and deveined

1 cup (130g) frozen peas

Sea salt

Black pepper

Juice of ½ lemon

Home from work and starving? This simple, but tasty, meal can be on the table in less than twenty minutes. The citrus flavors in the beer enhance the sweetness of the shrimp, and best of all, it uses less than a third of a bottle of Hop House 13 so there's enough left over for the chef.
Yield: 2 servings

Cook the spaghetti in a large saucepan of boiling salted water, according to package instructions until tender. Drain in a colander.

Meanwhile, in a large sauté pan or skillet (one that can hold the entire dish) over medium-high heat, melt 1 tablespoon (15g) of the butter. Add the garlic and chile, and cook for 2 to 3 minutes, until fragrant. Add the beer and bring to a boil.

Add the shrimp and peas, turn the heat to low, and simmer for about 3 minutes, until the shrimp turn pink. Add the remaining 1 tablespoon (15g) butter and simmer for 2 minutes more. Taste and season with salt, black pepper, and the lemon juice.

Add the pasta to the shrimp, tossing to coat. Serve immediately.

OPEN GATE BREWERY MARYLAND CRAB CAKES

Open Gate Brewery's Maryland Crab Cakes are true to Baltimore tradition, according to Executive Sous Chef Kamryn Dudley, due to "[having] a lot of crab, very little filler, and being broiled rather than fried." Of course, there's also a little seafood seasoning in the mix, alongside that local blue crab meat, to make it pure Baltimore. If you can't get your hands on Old Bay seasoning, try substituting J & O crab seasoning instead—or visit the Open Gate Brewery in Baltimore for a taste of the real thing.

Yield: 8 crab cakes

½ cup (115g) mayonnaise

1 large egg, beaten

1 tablespoon Dijon mustard

1 tablespoon Worcestershire sauce

½ teaspoon hot sauce

½ tablespoon seafood seasoning (e.g., Old Bay or similar brand)

1 pound (450g) jumbo lump crab meat, picked over

20 saltine crackers, finely crushed

¼ cup (60ml) canola oil

Lemon wedges, for serving

In a small bowl, whisk together the mayonnaise, egg, mustard, Worcestershire sauce, hot sauce, and seafood seasoning until smooth. In a medium bowl, lightly toss the crab meat with the cracker crumbs. Gently fold the crab mixture into the mayonnaise mixture. Cover and refrigerate for at least 1 hour.

Preheat the broiler on low and arrange a rack in the top third of the oven.

Scoop the crab mixture into eight ⅓-cup mounds. Use your fingers to lightly pack the mounds into patties about 1½ inches thick. Place the crab cakes onto a lightly oiled baking sheet, and place the sheet on the rack nearest the top of the oven. Broil the crab cakes until they are dark brown on top, approximately 8 to 10 minutes. Transfer the crab cakes to plates, and serve with lemon wedges and a glass of Hop House 13.

GUINNESS AND OYSTERS

The pairing of Guinness and oysters has been long celebrated in Ireland. Oysters have a central place in Irish food culture, with delicious homegrown delicacies widely consumed in restaurants, pubs, and market stalls, at festivals, and while visiting Ireland's dozens of oyster farms. These glistening beauties all have different characteristics: They take on and reflect the unique flavors and qualities from the marine environment in which they are grown.

So, how to pair oysters and Guinness? Always buy oysters unopened and get the freshest ones that you can. Many oyster farms offer overnight delivery for the best experience. Keep them chilled, then just before you want to eat, open, or "shuck," them:

- Fold a tea towel lengthwise into thirds.

- Place an oyster, rounded-side down, on the folded towel so that you can use the towel to prevent the shell from slipping around and protect your hand.

- Insert the point of a shucking knife into the hinge of the oyster shell.

- Twist and wriggle the knife to open the shell, then cut the muscle that connects the top and bottom shells.

- Pull the top shell off, then cut under the oyster to release it.

Serve the oysters raw on the half shell on a bed of crushed ice, with a squeeze of fresh lemon juice. The classic pairing is Guinness Draught and fresh oysters, but there's room to play.

CONTRAST: Pair oysters from different farms with the different stouts—Guinness Draught, Guinness Extra Stout, Guinness Foreign Extra Stout—and see which duo is your favorite

COMPLEMENT: Try oysters with a chilled glass of crisp, refreshing Hop House 13 or Baltimore Blonde for a pairing that complements the salty brine of the oysters, elevating their freshness with gentle hoppiness.

COOK: If the oysters are fried, pair them with Hop House 13 or Baltimore Blonde for something crisp to cut through that richness. Baked oysters, especially if they come with something unctuous like blue cheese, are an ideal pairing with Guinness Draught or Guinness Extra Stout, beers that won't overwhelm the oyster but play nicely with the cheese. If you've popped those oysters on the grill and included bacon in the action, pick a bottle of Guinness Foreign Extra Stout; the higher level of hops and alcohol will hold up well against the smoky flavors.

STEAMED MUSSELS IN HOP HOUSE 13

"Guinness is so good with seafood" declared adverts from the late 1950s. They weren't wrong. It's also good in seafood dishes, and mussels—cheap, sustainable, and easy to cook—are a great way to showcase this. Steam the mussels over Hop House 13 for an extra level of delicious hoppy flavor, and be sure to serve with plenty of fresh crusty bread for soaking up all the delicious broth. **Yield: 2 servings**

2¼ pounds (1kg) live mussels in shells

1 tablespoon extra-virgin olive oil

1 onion, halved and thinly sliced

2 garlic cloves, thinly sliced

Black pepper

2 tablespoons tomato paste

One 11.2-fluid-ounce (330ml) bottle Guinness Hop House 13 Lager or Guinness Baltimore Blonde Beer

Handful fresh basil leaves, shredded

Place the mussels in a large bowl of cold water. Using a small sharp knife, scrape off barnacles and remove any brown wispy bits (beards) that hang out of the shells. Discard any mussels with broken shells or those that do not close when tapped. Drain the mussels in a colander.

In a large saucepan over medium-high heat, heat the olive oil until it shimmers. Add the onion and garlic, season with black pepper (no salt, as the mussels come salted from the sea), and cook until the onion is softened, about 5 minutes. Add the tomato paste and cook, stirring often, for 2 minutes, then add the beer and simmer for 5 minutes, until slightly reduced.

Add the mussels, cover tightly, and turn the heat to medium. Steam for 5 to 6 minutes, shaking the pan halfway through, until the shells have opened. Discard any unopened mussels.

To serve, divide the mussels between two warm bowls, pouring over the pan juices, and sprinkle with basil.

STOUT AND MISO-GLAZED SALMON

Olive oil for greasing baking sheet

1 tablespoon barley miso

2 tablespoons Guinness Draught Stout

1 tablespoon maple syrup

1 tablespoon hot sauce, such as Hop House 13 Mango Hot Sauce (page 62)

½ inch (1cm) fresh ginger, peeled and grated

Juice of ½ lime

Four 5-ounce (140g) salmon fillets

2 scallions, white and green parts, thinly sliced

1 tablespoon sesame seeds, toasted

Lime wedges for serving

Barley miso, made with fermented barley and soybeans, has a longer fermentation time than white miso, creating a balance of sweet and savory that pairs perfectly with the bitterness of Guinness Draught. This glaze makes a simple portion of grilled fish feel like a luxurious treat. Serve with steamed rice and sesame oil–dressed greens.

Yield: 4 servings

Preheat the grill (broiler) to high heat with rack 4 inches (10cm) from the heating element. Line a rimmed baking sheet with aluminum foil and brush with olive oil.

In a small saucepan over medium heat, whisk together the miso, beer, maple syrup, hot sauce, and ginger. Bring to a simmer, then cook for 2 to 3 minutes, until the glaze has reduced slightly. Stir in the lime juice.

Place the fillets, skin-side up, on the prepared baking sheet, brush liberally with the glaze, and grill (broil) for 6 to 8 minutes, or until salmon is opaque and flakes easily with a fork.

Sprinkle the fish with the scallions and sesame seeds. Serve immediately with lime wedges on the side.

HOP HOUSE 13 LIME FISH TACOS

Adding Hop House 13 to the batter for these fish tacos brings another layer of flavor to the party. Accentuate the bright hoppy flavors by adding lots of lime to the crunchy salad. Heat the tortillas in a dry pan and keep them warm wrapped in a tea towel between two plates while you prepare the fish. **Yield: 4 servings**

SALAD

1 small red onion, halved and thinly sliced

1 jalapeño chile, seeded and thinly sliced

Juice of 2 limes

½ small red cabbage, finely shredded

Small bunch fresh cilantro (coriander), coarsely chopped

Fine sea salt

SAUCE

1 tablespoon chipotle paste or sriracha

½ cup (120g) sour cream

FISH

Vegetable oil for deep frying

1¾ cups (210g) all-purpose flour

½ teaspoon baking powder

¼ teaspoon sea salt

One 11.2-fluid-ounce (330ml) bottle Guinness Hop House 13 Lager or Guinness Baltimore Blonde Beer, very cold

14 ounces (400g) skinless whitefish fillets, such as cod, hake, or haddock, cut into strips

SERVING

Soft corn tortillas, warmed

Lime wedges (optional)

Sliced avocado (optional)

Tomato salsa (optional)

TO MAKE THE SALAD: In a salad bowl, soak the onion and jalapeño in the lime juice for 5 minutes, then add the cabbage and cilantro. Season with salt and toss well.

TO MAKE THE SAUCE: Stir together the chipotle paste and sour cream in a small bowl.

TO MAKE THE FISH: Heat 2 inches (5cm) of vegetable oil in a deep fryer, deep saucepan, or Dutch oven fitted with a fry thermometer to 365°F (185°C). Preheat the oven to 300°F (150°C).

Meanwhile, mix together the flour, baking powder, and salt in a large bowl, then whisk in the beer to make a smooth batter.

Working in batches, dip the fish strips in the batter, shaking off the excess, then carefully lower them into the oil. Fry until golden brown, about 2 to 3 minutes per side, then scoop them out with a slotted spoon and drain quickly on kitchen towels. Transfer them to the oven to keep warm until everything is cooked.

TO SERVE: Set bowls of crunchy salad, spicy sour cream, warm tortillas, and battered fish on the table so diners can construct their own tacos. Serve with lime, avocado, and salsa (if using).

DESSERTS
& BAKING

MALTED GUINNESS DRAUGHT NO-CHURN ICE CREAM

Once you've made this no-churn ice cream, with layers of flavor from the malted milk powder and Guinness Draught, you'll never want to go back to regular ice cream again. Save a little Guinness to make the most amazing ice cream float. **Yield: 2⅓ pints (1.1L)**

One 14.9-fluid-ounce (440ml) can Guinness Draught Stout, divided

One 14-ounce (400g) can condensed milk

¼ cup (30g) malted milk powder, such as Ovaltine

¼ teaspoon fine sea salt

2 cups (480ml) heavy cream

Pour 14 fluid ounces (400ml) of the beer into a small saucepan over medium-high heat, bring to a boil, then cook for 8 to 10 minutes, until reduced to about 3½ fluid ounces (100ml) in volume. Set aside to cool for 10 minutes.

In a large bowl, whisk together the condensed milk, malted milk powder, and salt. Add the reduced beer to the bowl, along with the remaining unreduced beer. Mix well.

In a separate bowl, whip the cream until soft peaks form. Pour the condensed milk mixture into the cream and gently mix until thoroughly combined.

Pour the ice cream base into a large airtight container and freeze for 6 to 8 hours, or overnight. Serve straight from the freezer.

OPEN GATE BREWERY FOREIGN EXTRA STOUT COOKIES

These delicious ultra chocolatey cookies were initially developed at the Open Gate Brewery during the early days of the COVID-19 pandemic. According to Executive Sous Chef Kamryn Dudley, the double dose of chocolate in the recipe was inspired by a doctor she knew who loved chocolate and "deserved every bit of spoiling at the time." The recipe kept evolving until it was perfect, and now these "pandemic cookies," as they're affectionately known by the culinary team, are a popular treat for brewery visitors year-round. **Yield: 12 to 15 cookies**

2 sticks (8 ounces [225g]) butter, at room temperature

¾ cup (150g) granulated sugar

¾ cup (165g) packed light brown sugar

2 large eggs

1 teaspoon vanilla extract

1 teaspoon Guinness Foreign Extra Stout

2¼ cups (270g) all-purpose flour

½ cup (45g) old fashioned rolled oats

2 tablespoons malted milk powder

1 teaspoon baking powder

1 teaspoon sea salt

¼ teaspoon ground cinnamon

2 cups (340g) semisweet chocolate chips

2 cups (340g) dark chocolate chunks

Flaky sea salt for sprinkling

Preheat the oven to 300°F (150°C).

In the bowl of a stand mixer fitted with a paddle attachment, cream the butter, granulated sugar, and brown sugar on medium speed for a full 3 to 4 minutes, until light and fluffy. With the machine still running, add the eggs, one a time, mixing until fully combined. Add the vanilla and stout, mixing until combined. Stop the mixer and scrape down the sides of the bowl.

Add the flour, oats, malted milk powder, baking powder, salt, and cinnamon. Mix on low speed until fully incorporated. Add the chocolate chips and chunks, and pulse the mixer on low until just mixed.

Place four ¼-cup scoops of cookie dough onto a rimmed baking sheet spaced well apart and sprinkle them with flaky sea salt. Bake for 15 minutes or until slightly brown around the edges. Let the cookies cool on the baking sheet for five minutes and then transfer to a wire rack to cool completely. Repeat with remaining dough and a cooled baking sheet.

PEANUT BUTTER AND STOUT SNACKING CAKE

Never had a peanut butter cup with a Guinness beer? You're missing out! Pairing that creamy, salty, sweet goodness with stout makes for a very special mouthful. Take it one step further by turning this happy combination into a simple snacking cake. **Yield: One 8-inch (20cm) square cake**

CAKE

1 stick (4 ounces [110g]) unsalted butter, melted

⅔ cup (140g) packed light brown sugar

½ cup (120g) smooth peanut butter

1 teaspoon vanilla extract

2 medium eggs

1 cup (120g) all-purpose flour

½ teaspoon baking powder

½ teaspoon sea salt

¼ cup (60ml) Guinness Extra Stout

GLAZE

⅓ cup (60ml) heavy cream

2 ounces (60g) 55% dark chocolate, chopped

Preheat the oven to 350°F (180°C). Butter and line an 8-inch (20cm) square baking pan with parchment paper.

TO MAKE THE CAKE: In a large bowl, using a wooden spoon, mix together the butter, brown sugar, peanut butter, and vanilla until well combined. Add the eggs, one at a time, mixing after each addition.

In a separate large bowl, sift together the flour, baking powder, and salt. Gently combine the flour mixture into the batter, then stir in the stout. Pour the batter into the prepared baking pan and bake for 18 to 20 minutes, or until a cake tester inserted in the center comes out clean.

Cool on a wire rack for 10 minutes before removing the cake from the pan and allowing to cool completely.

TO MAKE THE GLAZE: In a small saucepan over medium heat, heat the cream until it's just about to boil. Place the chocolate in a small bowl and add the hot cream. Whisk until the mixture is smooth and glossy, then pour over the cooled cake.

UPSIDE DOWN SPICED PEAR AND STOUT CAKE

This delectable mixture of warm spices and juicy pears needs the bitterness of Guinness Foreign Extra Stout to make sure the whole thing doesn't get too sweet.

Yield: One 10-inch (26cm) cake

Preheat the oven to 350°F (180°C).

TO MAKE THE TOPPING: In a small pan over medium heat, melt the butter. Stir in the light brown sugar, mixing well for 1 to 2 minutes. Transfer the butter mixture to a 10-inch (26cm) round springform pan and spread it across the base. Sprinkle with a pinch of salt. Arrange the pears, cut-side down, in a single layer on top.

TO MAKE THE CAKE: In a medium pan over medium heat, warm the stout, butter, and dark brown sugar together until the butter is melted. Remove the pan from the heat and pour the stout mixture into a large bowl to cool for 10 minutes. In a separate large bowl, sift together the flour, baking soda, ginger, mixed spice, cardamom, and salt.

Whisk the eggs into the cooled stout mixture, then fold in the flour mixture until just combined. Pour the batter carefully into the springform pan over the pears. Place the pan on a rimmed baking sheet (in case of leaks) and bake for 45 to 50 minutes, until a knife inserted into the center comes out clean.

Cool the cake in the pan for 10 minutes, then run a knife around the edge and—very carefully—invert the cake onto a serving plate. Serve warm.

TOPPING

4 tablespoons (60g) unsalted butter

½ cup (110g) packed light brown sugar

Pinch fine sea salt

Two 15-ounce (420g) cans pear halves, drained

CAKE

½ cup (120ml) Guinness Foreign Extra Stout

1 stick (4 ounces [110g]) unsalted butter

1 cup (240g) packed dark brown sugar

1¾ cups (210g) self-rising flour

1 teaspoon baking soda

1 teaspoon ground ginger

½ teaspoon mixed spice or pumpkin pie spice

¼ teaspoon ground cardamom

¼ teaspoon fine sea salt

3 eggs

TRADITIONAL IRISH PORTER CAKE

Visit any grandmother's house in Ireland, and you will find a porter cake, made with Guinness, in a tin somewhere in the kitchen. This version of the classic recipe includes a drizzle of Roe and Co. Irish whiskey over the cake when it comes out of the oven, adding an extra note of warm spice and fruit. **Yield: One 9-inch (23cm) cake**

1 cup plus 2 tablespoons (270ml) Guinness Draught Stout

1 cup (220g) packed light brown sugar

2 sticks (8 ounces [225g]) unsalted butter, plus more for greasing pan

1 pound 12 ounces (800g) mixed dried fruit, such as raisins, sultanas (golden raisins), and chopped prunes

4¾ cups (570g) all-purpose flour

½ teaspoon baking soda

¼ teaspoon fine sea salt

1½ teaspoons mixed spice or pumpkin pie spice

½ teaspoon freshly grated nutmeg

3 eggs, beaten

3 tablespoons Roe & Co. Blended Irish Whiskey (optional)

Preheat the oven to 325°F (160°C). Grease a 9-inch (23cm) round springform pan with butter and line it with parchment paper.

In a large saucepan over medium heat, combine the beer, sugar, and butter. Stirring frequently, heat until the butter is melted and the sugar is dissolved. Add the dried fruit and bring to a boil. Reduce the heat to low and simmer for 5 minutes, until the fruit is plump and soft. Remove the pan from the heat and transfer the fruit mixture to a large bowl to cool quickly.

In a medium bowl, sift together the flour, baking soda, salt, mixed spice, and nutmeg. Stir the eggs into the cooled fruit mixture, then add the flour mixture, mixing well to combine.

Scrape the batter into the prepared springform pan and bake for 1½ to 1¾ hours, or until the cake is well risen, dark golden brown, and a cake tester comes out clean from the center. Remove the pan from the oven and drizzle the whiskey (if using) on top while the cake is hot.

Cool the cake on a wire rack before removing it from the pan. Wrap it in parchment paper and store in an airtight container. Keep the cake for two to three days—if you can resist!—before serving it.

WHITE CHOCOLATE AND HOP HOUSE 13 CAKE WITH BROWN BUTTER GLAZE

On its own, white chocolate can be a little too sweet; the Hop House 13 in this recipe brings a welcome hint of bitterness to the cake. If you've ever watched any British baking competition, you will have heard of golden syrup, a sweet, smooth syrup that is often used in baking in Ireland and the United Kingdom. It's easy to find in the US, too—just take a look in the regular baking aisle, or the international aisle, at the grocery store.

Yield: One 5-by-9-inch (13-by-23cm) loaf cake

Preheat the oven to 340°F (170°C). Grease a 5-by-9 inch (13-by-23cm) loaf pan with butter and line it with parchment paper.

TO MAKE THE CAKE: In a heavy-bottom saucepan over medium heat, combine the butter, white chocolate, brown sugar, beer, and golden syrup. Stir for 5 minutes, or until everything has melted and the mixture is smooth. Set aside to cool for 15 minutes.

In a large bowl, sift together the flour, baking powder, and salt and set aside.

One at a time, add the eggs to the cooled beer-sugar mixture, beating well after each addition. Add the flour mixture and stir until well combined.

Pour the batter into the prepared pan and bake for 55 to 65 minutes or until a cake tester comes out clean from the center. Allow the cake to cool in the pan for 15 minutes before turning it out onto a wire rack to cool completely.

TO MAKE THE GLAZE: In a small saucepan over medium heat, melt the butter, stirring frequently, until it foams, turns golden brown, and smells nutty. This will take about 6 minutes.

Immediately pour the brown butter into a medium bowl. Whisk in the icing sugar, vanilla, and 1 tablespoon of milk, adding more milk as necessary to create a pouring consistency.

Pour the glaze over the cooled cake at once, allowing the glaze to drip down the sides. Serve.

CAKE

1¾ sticks (7 ounces [200g]) unsalted butter, plus more for greasing pan

7 ounces (200g) white chocolate

1¼ cups (200g) packed dark brown sugar

¾ cup (180ml) Guinness Hop House 13 Lager or Guinness Baltimore Blonde Beer

1 tablespoon golden syrup

2½ cups (300g) all-purpose flour

1 teaspoon baking powder

½ teaspoon fine sea salt

2 eggs

GLAZE

4 tablespoons (60g) unsalted butter

1½ cups (180g) icing (powdered) sugar, sifted

2 teaspoons vanilla extract

1 to 3 tablespoons milk

GUINNESS AND CHOCOLATE

Guinness and chocolate make a beautiful couple. Both halves of this delicious duo of fermented foods rely on the delicate balance of sweet and bitter for their sophisticated appeal. When they come together, it's magical. A touch of beer bitterness can elevate a chocolate dish from the mundane to the irresistible.

One of the best ways to explore how well they go together is by gathering a selection of your favorite chocolate bars (in different cocoa percentages) and a few bottles of Guinness and inviting some friends over for a beer and chocolate evening. There's a wonderful synergy to the best pairings. Try something like a rich, fruity 70% dark Ecuadorian chocolate, with coffee and roasted malt flavors, and a glass of Foreign Extra Stout, and see how each highlights something in the other.

When baking with chocolate, Guinness brings several things to the table: It deepens and intensifies the chocolate flavor, the bitter beer acts as a counterpoint to sugar in the recipe, and the extra liquid makes cakes and bakes more deliciously moist.

For baking, stouts are the obvious pairing with dark chocolate. The sweetness in chocolate brings out the bitterness in beer, along with its roasted malt, coffee, and chocolate flavors. In turn, the beer enhances the cocoa and chocolate in cakes, brownies, and truffles. The ales and lagers have their own role to play with white chocolate, the hoppy notes making sure that the cocoa butter sweetness never becomes too cloying.

GUINNESS DRAUGHT CHEESECAKE BROWNIES

This simple brownie recipe is one of the best ways to showcase the perfect match of Guinness and chocolate. No one can resist beer brownies, especially when they're topped with a white mascarpone cheesecake, a creamy visual callout to the head on a good pint of Guinness beer. **Yield: 30 pieces**

CHEESECAKE TOPPING

9 ounces (250g) mascarpone cheese, at room temperature

1 medium egg

½ teaspoon vanilla extract

¼ cup (50g) granulated or caster sugar

BROWNIES

1 cup (120g) all-purpose flour

⅔ cup (60g) Dutch-processed cocoa powder

¼ teaspoon sea salt

½ teaspoon baking powder

6 ounces (170g) 55% dark chocolate, chopped

1½ sticks (6 ounces [170g]) unsalted butter

1 cup (200g) granulated or caster sugar

2 medium eggs

½ teaspoon vanilla extract

1 cup (240ml) Guinness Draught Stout

Preheat the oven to 350°F (180°C). Line a 10½-by-8-inch (27-by-20cm) baking pan with parchment paper.

TO MAKE THE CHEESECAKE TOPPING: In a medium bowl, whisk together the mascarpone, egg, vanilla, and sugar until well combined. Set aside.

TO MAKE THE BROWNIES: In a medium bowl, sift together the flour, cocoa powder, salt, and baking powder. Set aside.

In a large saucepan over low heat, gently melt the chocolate and butter together. Remove the pan from the heat and transfer the chocolate mixture to a large bowl. Add the sugar, whisking until smooth. Allow to cool slightly, then whisk in the eggs, vanilla, and beer. Whisk in the flour mixture until just combined. The batter will be quite runny.

Pour the batter into the prepared pan. Dot the cheesecake topping across the top, then use a knife to swirl with abandon.

Bake for 23 to 25 minutes, until the brownies are set and a cake tester inserted into the center comes out clean. Cool the brownies completely in the pan before cutting into 30 pieces. Serve at room temperature

CHOCOLATE, STOUT, AND POTATO CAKE

CAKE

2 sticks (8 ounces [225g])
unsalted butter, at room
temperature, plus more
for greasing pan

1 cup (200g) granulated
or caster sugar

1 cup (220g) packed light
muscovado sugar

4 medium eggs, at
room temperature

4 ounces (90g) 70% dark
chocolate, broken into
pieces and melted

⅓ cup (70g) leftover
mashed potato

2 cups (240g) all-purpose flour

⅓ cup (30g) Dutch-processed
cocoa powder

1 teaspoon baking powder

½ teaspoon baking soda

½ cup plus 2 tablespoons
(150ml) Guinness Foreign
Extra Stout

ICING

1 stick (4 ounces [110g])
unsalted butter, at
room temperature

1½ cups (180g) icing
(powdered) sugar, sifted

One 8-ounce (225g)
package cream cheese,
at room temperature

1 teaspoon vanilla extract

Pinch sea salt

Guinness is, first and foremost, an Irish beer, and in Ireland, we have a true respect for the potato. You don't just buy a bag of generic spuds; you choose between varieties depending on how you're going to cook them. Each household has their opinions and favorites, debating Cara versus Golden Wonder, Maris Piper over Rooster, Kerr's Pink or Home Guard. This recipe, which gets extra richness from Foreign Extra Stout, makes it easy: Just have your favorite mashed potato for dinner and save some for the cake. **Yield: One 7-inch (18cm) round tiered cake**

Preheat the oven to 350°F (180°C). Grease three 7-inch (18cm) round cake pans with butter and line them with parchment paper.

TO MAKE THE CAKE: In the bowl of a stand mixer fitted with a paddle attachment, cream the butter, caster sugar, and muscovado sugar together for 3 to 4 minutes, until light and fluffy. Add the eggs, one at a time, beating well after each addition. Mix in the melted chocolate and mashed potato.

In a separate large bowl, sift together the flour, cocoa powder, baking powder, and baking soda. Working in three additions, gently mix the flour mixture into the butter-sugar mixture, adding a third of the beer after each addition.

Divide the batter evenly among the prepared pans and bake for 20 to 25 minutes, or until the cakes feel springy and a cake tester comes out clean from the center. Cool in the pans for 10 minutes, then turn the cakes onto a wire rack and allow to cool completely.

TO MAKE THE ICING: In a medium bowl, beat the butter and icing sugar together until smooth, then mix in the cream cheese, vanilla, and salt until well combined.

Put the first cake layer on a serving platter and use an offset spatula to spread with ¾ cup (170g) of icing. Top with another cake layer and spread with ¾ cup (170g) of icing. Top with the remaining cake layer and spread the remaining icing across the top of the cake.

Chill in the fridge for 1 hour to set the icing. Store for several days in an airtight container in the fridge, but bring to room temperature before serving.

EXTRA STOUT-SOAKED CHRISTMAS PUDDING

1⅓ cups (230g) currants

1½ cups (240g) sultanas (golden raisins)

1½ cups (240g) raisins

1 cup (220g) packed light brown sugar

1 tablespoon black treacle or molasses

2 tablespoons Roe & Co. Blended Irish Whiskey

Zest and juice of 1 orange

⅔ cup (160ml) Guinness Extra Stout

1½ sticks (6 ounces [170g]) unsalted butter, melted, plus more for greasing bowls

⅓ cup (60g) chopped candied citrus peel of your choice

1 apple, peeled, cored, and grated

3 medium eggs, beaten

2 cups (170g) fresh bread crumbs

1 cup (120g) self-rising flour

1 teaspoon mixed spice or pumpkin pie spice

½ teaspoon freshly grated nutmeg

¼ teaspoon sea salt

Brandy butter for serving

SPECIAL SUPPLIES
Steamer

Guinness has had pride of place in Christmas food for many years, with recipes in the Guinness archives from 1955 giving directions on "how to make a Christmas cake with Guinness" and a recipe for "Gold Medal Christmas Pudding" featured in a booklet from the previous year. We've amped up the flavors by using Guinness Extra Stout along with some Roe and Co. Irish whiskey. The perfect pudding for Stir-up Sunday, the last Sunday before Advent, which normally falls toward the end of November, this festive treat is best made in advance.
Yield: Two 2-pint (1L) puddings, each serving 6 to 8

In a very large bowl, combine the currants, sultanas, raisins, and brown sugar. Add the treacle, whiskey, orange zest and juice, and stout, and mix well. Cover and leave the fruit to soak overnight, or for up to 24 hours, at room temperature.

The next day, grease two 2-pint (1L) pudding bowls with butter.

Mix the melted butter, candied peel, apple, eggs, and bread crumbs into the soaked fruit mixture. In a separate large bowl, sift together the flour, mixed spice, nutmeg, and salt. Add the flour mixture to the fruit mixture and stir until everything is well combined.

Pack the pudding mixture into the prepared bowls and cover with a double layer of parchment paper and a sheet of aluminum foil. Tie the coverings securely around the rims of the pudding bowls with string. You want to make sure that steam can't get into the pudding.

Bring a large saucepan of water to a simmer over medium heat. Add a steamer on top, making sure the water does not touch the bottom. Add the puddings, cover, and steam for 6 hours, adding boiling water as necessary so the pan does not boil dry. It's a good idea to set an alarm so that you check it every 45 minutes.

Remove the pudding from the steamer and cool completely. Store in a cool place until needed. To reheat, steam again for another 2 hours before serving hot with brandy butter on the side.

COCOA-DUSTED FOREIGN EXTRA STOUT TRUFFLES

½ **cup (55g) packed light muscovado sugar**

½ **cup (120g) Guinness Foreign Extra Stout**

10 ounces (280g) 60% dark chocolate, chopped

½ **cup (45g) Dutch-processed cocoa powder for dusting**

Homemade truffles are incredibly easy to make and irresistible to eat! Pack these into a cute box to make a lovely gift for the Guinness-lover in your life. **Yield: 30 to 40 truffles**

Line a 4-by-8 inch (10-by-20cm) loaf pan with parchment paper.

Heat the sugar and stout together in a small saucepan over medium heat until the sugar is melted. Bring to a simmer.

Place the chocolate in a medium bowl. Add the hot liquid and whisk by hand until the chocolate is melted and the mixture is smooth. Pour the chocolate mixture into the loaf pan and refrigerate for 1 to 2 hours, or until solid.

Sift the cocoa powder into a shallow bowl. Using the parchment paper, lift the truffle loaf out of the pan and cut it into teaspoon-size cubes. Working in small batches, roll the truffles in the cocoa powder.

Store in an airtight container in the fridge for up to two weeks. These are best served at room temperature.

DUBLIN GUINNESS STOREHOUSE CHOCOLATE MOUSSE

This chocolate mousse recipe from Dublin's Guinness Storehouse is a true delight. According to Chef Sean Hunter, "the roasted barley makes the chocolate taste more pronounced, the hops add a bitter dimension to the dish, which adds depth of flavor, and the creamy smooth nitrogen bubbles help aerate the mixture for a lighter consistency and a more decadent mouthfeel in the final mousse." Chef Sean Hunter says customers "are really amazed by this food and beer pairing and how well Guinness works with chocolate." **Yield: 5 servings**

9 medium egg whites, at room temperature

½ teaspoon lemon juice

Pinch sea salt

¼ cup (50g) caster (superfine) sugar

7.5 ounces (210g) 70% dark chocolate

¼ cup (60ml) Guinness Draught Stout

Whipped cream, for serving

SPECIAL SUPPLIES
Guinness half-pint glasses (optional)

In the bowl of a stand mixer fitted with a whisk attachment, whisk together the egg whites, lemon juice, and salt until soft peaks begin to form. Gradually add the sugar, whisking continuously, until stiff peaks begin to form.

Bring 1 to 2 inches (3 to 5cm) of water to a boil in small saucepan over medium-high heat. Place a small metal bowl on top of the pan, making sure the water doesn't touch the bottom. Add the chocolate and stir until it melts. When the chocolate is fully melted, slowly add the beer, stirring to combine.

Remove the pan from the heat and quickly but gently whisk in one-third of the egg white mixture. This will create a looser mixture that is easier to work with.

Gently fold in the remaining egg white mixture with a spatula until fully combined. Be careful not to knock the air out of the mixture. You should have a lovely light, glossy mousse.

Serve in Guinness half-pints, if you have them. Top with a healthy serving of whipped cream. They'll look like mini Guinnesses!

SALTED CARAMEL AND CHOCOLATE GUINNESS DRAUGHT TART

The salt-malt flavor of the pretzel crust in this tart contrasts with the sweetness of the caramel and enhances the flavor of Guinness in the chocolate ganache. Serve in thin slices—it's rich!—with some softly whipped cream. **Yield: One 10-inch (25cm) tart**

CRUST

1½ **cups (180g) small salted pretzels**

6 **tablespoons (90g) unsalted butter, melted, plus more for greasing pan**

¼ **cup (55g) packed light brown sugar**

FILLING

One 14-ounce (400g) can caramel or dulce de leche

½ **teaspoon fine sea salt**

¾ **cup plus 1 tablespoon (195ml) heavy cream**

10 **ounces (280g) 55% dark chocolate, chopped**

⅓ **cup (80ml) Guinness Draught Stout**

Preheat the oven to 350°F (180°C). Grease a 10-inch (25cm) tart pan with a removable base with butter.

TO MAKE THE CRUST: Put the pretzels in the bowl of a food processor. Blitz until they turn into rough crumbs. Add the butter and brown sugar and blitz until the mixture is well combined and starts to clump. Transfer the mixture to the prepared pan and, using the base of a straight-sided measuring cup, press evenly across the base and up the sides of the pan to form a crust.

Bake for 15 minutes, until dark golden. Set aside to cool completely.

TO MAKE THE FILLING: In a small bowl, whisk together the caramel and salt, then spoon it into the tart base. Gently spread to cover the base evenly.

In a small saucepan over medium heat, heat the cream until it's just about to boil. Add the chocolate into a medium bowl and add the hot cream. Whisk by hand until the chocolate is melted and the mixture is silky smooth. Whisk in the beer and gently pour the chocolate-beer mixture over the caramel.

Place the tart in the fridge for at least 1 hour to set. If you wish to live dangerously, you can carefully remove the tart from the pan before serving.

TIP To make your own caramel for this tart, all you need is a can of condensed milk. Remove the label. Fill a deep medium saucepan with water and place the unopened can in the saucepan, covering it by 2 inches (5cm) with water. This will prevent the can from overheating. Make sure there's enough water to completely cover the can at all times, topping up frequently during the cooking process. Simmer, uncovered, for 3 hours, checking every 30 minutes. Carefully remove the hot can from the simmering water using tongs. Allow to cool completely before opening.

HOP HOUSE 13 BURNT HONEYCOMB CINDER TOFFEE

1 cup (200g) caster or granulated sugar

¾ cup (165g) packed light brown sugar

¼ cup (60ml) Guinness Hop House 13 Lager or Guinness Baltimore Blonde Beer

3 tablespoons (60g) honey

1 tablespoon (15g) unsalted butter, diced, plus more for greasing foil

¼ teaspoon fine sea salt

1 tablespoon baking soda

SPECIAL SUPPLIES
Candy thermometer

When baking soda meets hot sugar syrup, there's a volcanic eruption, creating the bubbles that make this sweet treat so irresistible. It's a little bit of science and a whole lot of magic, but the Hop House 13 makes sure that the result doesn't become too cloying. **Yield: 10 to 12 servings.**

Line a 9-by-13-inch (23-by-33cm) rimmed baking sheet with aluminum foil, then grease the foil with butter.

In a deep, heavy-bottom pan (this mixture foams up!) over low heat, combine the caster sugar, brown sugar, beer, honey, butter, and salt. Stir until melted, then turn the heat up to medium and bring to a simmer.

Simmer for about 10 to 15 minutes, until the mixture turns the color of maple syrup and a candy thermometer placed in the mixture reads 300°F (150°C). This is also known as the hard crack stage. Remove from the heat immediately. Quickly and carefully beat in the baking soda with a wooden spoon, minding your hand as it froths up.

Pour the toffee onto the prepared baking sheet, tilting the sheet from side to side to encourage the toffee to spread out.

Leave to cool before breaking the toffee into pieces and storing in an airtight container for up to one week.

HOT HONEY HOP HOUSE 13 BREAD

Hot honey, aka chile honey butter, is the secret ingredient in this bread that brings it from good to great. We recommend harissa, the multilayered North African chile paste, for this because it gives flecks of color to the bread. In a pinch, use sriracha instead. Give it a lift with Hop House 13 and enjoy!

Yield: One 4-by-8-inch (10-by-20cm) loaf

4 tablespoons (60g) salted butter, melted

2 teaspoons honey

1 tablespoon harissa

2¾ cups (330g) self-rising flour

1 teaspoon fine sea salt

One 11.2-fluid-ounce (330ml) bottle Guinness Hop House 13 Lager or Guinness Baltimore Blonde Beer

Salted butter for serving

Preheat the oven to 350°F (180°C) and line a 4-by-8-inch (10-by-20cm) loaf pan with parchment paper.

In a medium bowl, whisk together the butter, honey, and harissa until smooth. Set aside.

In a large bowl, sift together the flour and salt. Make a well in the center, pour in the beer and two-thirds of the hot honey, and stir gently with a wooden spoon until the batter is just combined.

Transfer the batter into the prepared pan, drizzle the remaining third of hot honey on top, and bake for 50 to 60 minutes, until a cake tester inserted into the center comes out clean and the base sounds hollow when tapped.

Remove the loaf from the pan and cool for a bit on a wire rack. This bread is best eaten warm, with plenty of salted butter.

GUINNESS IN BREAD

Beer has been used in bread baking for centuries, with bakers using the barm— the froth of fermenting beer—to rise their loaves before the advent of industrial yeast. These days, you're more likely to head to a grocery store to pick up a packet of instant yeast than go to St. James's Gate Brewery for barm, but even so, Guinness does give a lift to your loaf.

When used in quick breads, beer's yeast and carbonation works with baking powder to start the mixture rising immediately, helping to lighten the texture of the bread. If you need to have bread on the table and don't have any yeast on hand, easy Hot Honey Hop House 13 Bread (above) or Dublin Guinness Storehouse Soda Bread (page 119) are the fastest ones to make.

Using beer in yeast bread also gives more rise. The Cocoa, Stout, and Fig Loaf (page 125) takes less time to prove, and Guinness gives it a light texture as well as a deeper, richer flavor.

COCOA, STOUT, AND FIG LOAF

3⅓ cups (400g) strong white bread flour

1 cup (90g) Dutch-processed cocoa powder

1½ teaspoons fine sea salt

Two ¼-ounce (7g) packets instant dry yeast

2 tablespoons dark brown sugar

One 11.2-fluid-ounce (330ml) bottle Guinness Extra Stout

¼ cup (60ml) milk

7 ounces (200g) dried figs, stemmed and coarsely chopped (approximately 16 dried figs)

More savory than sweet, this bread pairs wonderfully with cheese. Top slices with soft goat cheese, drizzle with honey, and toast under the grill (broiler) for a simple lunch. It's also fantastic at breakfast when toasted, buttered, and spread with bitter orange marmalade.
Yield: One 10-inch (25cm) loaf

In a large bowl, whisk together the flour, cocoa powder, salt, yeast, and brown sugar. Make a well in the center and pour in the stout and milk. Mix together to form a stiff, slightly sticky dough.

Lightly flour a rimmed baking sheet and a work surface. Turn out the dough onto the work surface and knead for about 10 minutes, until it is smooth and silky. Knead in the figs until evenly distributed.

Leave the dough to rise in a clean bowl, covered by a tea towel, until doubled in size, about 1 hour. Gently deflate the dough and shape it into a long loaf, about 10 inches (25cm) in length. Transfer to the prepared baking sheet and cover with a tea towel. Prove in a warm place until almost doubled in size, about 45 minutes.

Preheat the oven to 425°F (220°C).

With a sharp knife, make three diagonal slashes across the top of the loaf. Bake for 45 minutes to 1 hour, until the loaf sounds hollow when tapped on the base. Cool on a wire rack.

SAVORY
HOP HOUSE 13
LOAF CAKE
WITH SALAMI AND SMOKED SCAMORZA

2 cups (240g) all-purpose flour

1 tablespoon baking powder

4 ounces (110g) salami, chopped

4 ounces (110g) smoked scamorza, chopped

4 medium eggs

½ cup (120ml) Guinness Hop House 13 Lager or Guinness Baltimore Blonde Beer

½ cup (120ml) extra-virgin olive oil

¼ cup (60ml) plain natural yogurt

1 teaspoon sea salt

Black pepper

The mixture of hoppy Hop House 13, meaty salami, and smoked scamorza (a semisoft Italian white cheese) is like a picnic packed into a loaf. Take it with you for outdoor eating or enjoy it indoors with a bowl of creamy tomato soup. **Yield: One 5-by-9-inch (13-by-23cm) loaf**

Preheat the oven to 350°F (180°C). Line a 5-by-9-inch (13-by-23cm) loaf pan with parchment paper.

In a large bowl, mix together the flour, baking powder, salami, and scamorza. In a separate large bowl, whisk together the eggs, beer, olive oil, and yogurt. Season well with the salt and black pepper. Add the flour mixture, stirring gently until just combined.

Scrape the batter into the prepared pan and bake for 30 to 40 minutes, or until a cake tester inserted into the center comes out clean (try to avoid the cheese and salami when testing this). Cool in the pan before enjoying.

COCKTAILS

Whether you're looking for something classy (let me get you a Black Velvet, page 130) or a pitcher of something refreshing (anyone want a Clara con Limón, page 130), beer cocktails are here to play. Here are eight simple cocktails that focus on the flavors and textures of Guinness and offer an array of options for any special occasion, event, or end-of-the-day happy hour.

BLACK VELVET

STOUT AND STORMY

BEERMOSA

AMARO SPRITZ

CLARA CON LIMÓN

AMARO SPRITZ

Yield: 1 serving

3 fluid ounces (90ml) Guinness Hop House 13 Lager or Guinness Baltimore Blonde Beer

2 fluid ounces (60ml) amaro

½ lemon for squeezing

1 lemon twist

Fill a large wineglass with cracked ice. Pour the beer over the ice, followed by the amaro. Squeeze in a little lemon juice, stir gently, and garnish with the lemon twist. Enjoy.

BEERMOSA

Yield: 2 servings

One 11.2-fluid-ounce (330ml) bottle Guinness Hop House 13 Lager or Guinness Baltimore Blonde Beer, chilled

Orange juice, chilled

Divide the beer between two champagne flutes. Carefully fill the glasses to the top with orange juice. Enjoy.

BLACK VELVET

Yield: 1 serving

2 fluid ounces (60ml) Guinness Draught Stout, chilled

2 fluid ounces (60ml) champagne, chilled

Pour the beer into a champagne glass. Carefully top up with champagne. Enjoy.

BITTER HOP HOUSE 13

Yield: 1 serving

1 fluid ounce (30ml) bitter red liqueur of choice

5 fluid ounces (150ml) Guinness Hop House 13 Lager or Guinness Baltimore Blonde Beer

Sparkling orange juice

1 orange twist

Put three ice cubes into a rocks glass. Pour the red liqueur into the glass, then add the beer. Top off with a splash of sparkling orange juice. Rub the rim of glass with the orange twist and drop it into the drink. Enjoy.

CLARA CON LIMÓN

Yield: 4 servings

Two 11.2-fluid-ounce (330ml) bottles Guinness Hop House 13 Lager or Guinness Baltimore Blonde Beer

22 fluid ounces (650ml) lemonade

Lemon slices for serving

Fresh mint for serving

Pour the beer into a large chilled pitcher. Slowly pour the lemonade on top of the beer. Stir, then serve in chilled beer mugs, garnished with a lemon slice and sprig of fresh mint. Enjoy.

ESPRESSO STOUT MARTINI

Yield: 2 servings

2 fluid ounces (60ml) spiced rum

2 fluid ounces (60ml) cold espresso

2 fluid ounces (60ml) crème de cacao

4 fluid ounces (120ml) Guinness Foreign Extra Stout

4 coffee beans

Put two martini glasses in the fridge to chill. Pour the rum into a pitcher with a handful of ice, then add the espresso, crème de cacao, and stout. Stir with a long spoon until the outside of the pitcher feels icy cold. Strain into the chilled glasses. Garnish each glass with two coffee beans. Enjoy.

SPICY GINGER SHANDY

Yield: 4 servings

1 lemon, thinly sliced

1 inch (2.5cm) fresh ginger, peeled and thinly sliced

2 ounces (60ml) ginger wine

Two 11.2-fluid-ounce (330ml) bottles Guinness Hop House 13 Lager or Guinness Baltimore Blonde Beer, chilled

One 12-fluid-ounce (350ml) bottle ginger beer

In a large pitcher, combine the lemon, fresh ginger, and ginger wine. Pour in the beer and ginger beer, stirring carefully. Fill four rocks glasses with ice, then pour in the shandy. Enjoy.

STOUT AND SPICE

Yield: 2 servings

4 fluid ounces (120ml) spiced rum

2 fluid ounces (60ml) fresh lime juice

One 11.2-fluid-ounce (330ml) bottle Guinness Extra Stout, very cold

2 lime wedges

In a large pitcher, combine the rum, lime juice, and stout, stirring gently. Fill two highball glasses with ice and divide the mixture between them. Garnish each glass with a wedge of lime. Enjoy.

GLOSSARY

ABV: Also known as alcohol by volume, ABV is a standard worldwide measurement of how much alcohol (ethanol) is in a drink. It is expressed as a percentage (e.g., 4.2% ABV). The higher the ABV, the more alcohol there is in a beverage.

Ale: A type of beer brewed with top-fermenting yeast at warm temperatures. Ales have distinctive fruity flavors.

Barley: A hardy cereal grain that is the main ingredient in beer.

Barley, pearl: A grain that has a distinctive chewy texture and nutty flavor. Pearl barley used for cooking is pale and creamy in color and can be used in dishes like salads, soups, stews, and risottos.

Barley, roasted: Unmalted barley, roasted to a high temperature, which gives Guinness its distinctive flavor.

Beer: A generic term for any drink made from fermented grains.

Black pudding: A mixture of pigs' blood— a plentiful and sustainable byproduct of the pork industry—fat, oatmeal, and spices packed into a sausage casing. Black pudding is a regional specialty in Ireland and the UK. Similar examples are also found in France (boudin noir), Spain (morcilla), Portugal (morcela), and Mexico (moronga).

Brewhouse: A name used for the set of vessels used in the production of beer.

Butter: When in doubt, add butter! Unsalted butter is the most versatile type for baking, as it is easier to control the amount of salt you add to a dish. Salted butter is good for cooking and perfect for spreading.

Carbon dioxide: A gas produced by yeast during fermentation. It is also one of the gases used to create the bubbles in your beer.

Carbonation: The process of putting fizz— carbon dioxide—in beer. These are the bubbles that refresh your palate when you're enjoying beer with food. Sometimes nitrogenation (nitrogen gas) is used to put fizz into stouts.

Cartouche: A piece of parchment paper that sits directly on the surface of a stew, sauce, or soup while it cooks. It is also known as a "false lid" and it serves multiple purposes: traps steam, reduces evaporation, keeps components submerged during cooking, and prevents a film from forming on the surface. Create a cartouche by cutting a large square out of parchment paper with scissors. Fold the square in half diagonally, joining opposite corners to make a triangle. Fold the triangle in half three more times, always folding along the long side, until you have a small triangle of parchment paper. Hold the folded triangle over your pot, pan, or dish with the point in the exact center of the vessel. Make a small mark with a pencil on the parchment paper where the edge of the vessel sits. Use scissors to trim the parchment paper at that mark, rounding the edge as much as possible. Snip off the tip of the triangle. When you unfold your paper, you should have a circle close to the exact size of your dish with a hole in the middle.

Deep frying: Cooking food by submerging it in a deep pan of hot oil. Deep frying is extremely fast and effective but can also be dangerous. Only use oil suitable for deep frying, like sunflower oil or peanut oil. Never fill the pan more than half full of oil, only fry a few pieces of food at a time, and never, ever leave a pan of hot oil unattended.

Digital kitchen scale: A inexpensive piece of kitchen equipment that lets you accurately measure dry, liquid, and chopped ingredients by weight. Put a bowl on the scale, use the tare button to set the scale to zero, and simply add the ingredient to measure. If you need more ingredients in the bowl, just set the scale to zero and repeat. It's fast and easy, and there are fewer utensils used, which means less washing up. Better baking and less mess. A win all round.

Draught beer: Beer that is served from a tap, normally in a pub or bar.

Dry Irish stout: A type of dark beer made with roasted barley, with a bitter, dry, roasted flavor.

Dulse: An edible seaweed that looks like red leafy lettuce when it's raw. Dulse has been a popular snack in Ireland and Scotland for generations. Full of vitamins and minerals and with a salty umami flavor, dulse makes a tasty addition to breads and scones. Buy dried flakes from well-stocked grocery stores.

Ethanol: Also known as alcohol, ethanol is one of the two main products of fermentation, along with carbon dioxide. ABV measures the amount of ethanol in beer.

Extra Stout: A type of beer. Guinness Extra Stout was first brewed in 1821 as a bottled product and is described as being "closest to the porter originally brewed by Arthur Guinness."

Fermentation: The process where sugars are converted by yeast into alcohol and carbon dioxide.

Flour: Flour types are defined by protein content, which influences how much gluten can be formed and determines the structure and texture of baked goods. If a flour has low protein, it will have less gluten. More protein means more gluten. The flours used in this book include:

> **Bread flour:** 12% to 14% protein. Best for yeast breads and pizza.
> **All-purpose flour:** 9% to 12% protein. Best for general use in cakes, brownies, muffins, batters, and sauces.
> **Self-rising flour:** 8.5% to 9.2% protein. Baking powder and salt are premixed into this flour. Best for quick breads, flatbreads, scones, batters, and cakes.
> **Rye flour:** 8% to 12% protein. Milled from rye berries or kernels, rye flour has a nutty flavor. Best for crispbreads and yeast breads.
> **Whole wheat flour:** 11% to 15% protein. With a rich flavor and coarse texture, whole wheat flour adds color, fiber, and nutrients to baking. Best for soda and yeast breads.

Foreign Extra Stout: A type of beer. A stronger stout brewed for the export market. Guinness Foreign Extra Stout, initially known as West India Porter, was first brewed at St. James's Gate Brewery in 1801. It's very popular in Asia, Africa, and the Caribbean.

Head: The fluffy foam on top of your beer.

Hops: The cone-shaped flowers of a plant called *Humulus lupulus.* Hops add bitterness, aroma, and flavor to beer, and they help preserve it.

Lager: A type of beer that is cold-fermented and cold-aged. Light and refreshing, lager is one of the world's most popular beer styles.

GLOSSARY (CONT.)

Malt: Malted barley, or malt, is the main ingredient in almost every beer. Barley is soaked in water to make it germinate, activating enzymes that convert starch reserves and proteins into sugars. The process is then stopped by heat.

Malthouse: Where barley is malted.

Mandoline: A mandoline slicer is the key to getting thin, even slices of vegetables like potatoes. But beware: They can cause severe cuts. Never use one without a hand guard, and always be cautious when handling the blades.

Miso: This fermented soybean paste is a staple in Japanese cooking. It has a deep umami, savory flavor that adds richness to many dishes.

Nitrogen: A gas sometimes used to put the fizz in stouts. It is also used to dispense these stouts from kegs. The nitrogen gas provides a smooth texture and creates a firm, creamy head.

Porter: A type of dark beer that was first brewed in England in the 1700s, before coming to Ireland and being brewed by Arthur Guinness.

Scald: To heat a liquid—usually milk—to just below the boiling point. Tiny bubbles will appear at the edge of the pan.

Smoked scamorza: This semisoft Italian white cheese is a close relative of mozzarella. It has a delicate smoky flavor and smooth texture.

Stout: A type of beer. Originally called stout (strong) porter, Guinness is the most famous of this type.

Widget: A floating device found in your can of Guinness Draught. The widget uses a nitrogen-filled capsule that is released when the can is opened to create a smooth, creamy head on your pint.

Yeast: A single-cell microorganism that causes fermentation in brewing, turning sugar into alcohol and carbon dioxide.

Yeast, instant dry: A dry yeast for baking that has smaller granules than active dry yeast and can be mixed directly into dry ingredients. Instant dry yeast is also known as quick-rise yeast or fast-acting yeast.

MEASUREMENT CONVERSION TABLES

All conversions are approximations. Do not alternate between different measurements within a recipe. For best results, we strongly recommend that all ingredients are weighed on a digital kitchen scale.

VOLUME: US TO METRIC (APPROXIMATE)

1 teaspoon = 5ml

1 tablespoon = 15ml

1 fluid ounce = 30ml

¼ cup = 60ml

⅓ cup = 80ml

3.4 fluid ounces = 100ml

½ cup = 120ml

¾ cup = 180ml

1 cup = 240ml

1 pint (2 cups) = 480ml

1 quart (4 cups) = 0.95L

WEIGHT: US TO METRIC (APPROXIMATE)

1 ounce = 28g

4 ounces = 110g

8 ounces = 225g

1 pound = 450g

TEMPERATURE (APPROXIMATE)

325°F = 160°C

350°F = 180°C

375°F = 190°C

400°F = 200°C

425°F = 220°C

450°F = 230°C

475°F = 240°C

INGREDIENTS (APPROXIMATE)

Barley: 1 cup = 200g

Bread crumbs: 1 cup = 85g

Butter: 1 tablespoon = 15g

Candied peel: 1 cup = 170g

Cheese, cheddar (grated):
   1 cup = 100g

Cheese, gruyère (grated):
   1 cup = 100g

Cheese, mozzarella (grated):
   1 cup = 115g

Chocolate chips: 1 cup = 170g

Chocolate chunks: 1 cup = 170g

Cocoa powder: 1 cup = 90g

Coconut oil: 1 cup = 200g

Coffee, ground: 1 cup = 80g

Currants: 1 cup = 175g

Flour, all-purpose: 1 cup = 120g

Flour, rye: 1 cup = 105g

Flour, self-rising: 1 cup = 120g

Flour, strong white bread:
   1 cup = 120g

Flour, whole wheat: 1 cup = 110g

Frosting: 1 cup = 230g

Honey: 1 cup = 320g
   1 tablespoon = 20g

Malted milk powder:
   1 cup = 120g

Maple syrup: 1 cup = 340g

Mayonnaise: 1 cup = 230g

Molasses: 1 cup = 340g

Mustard seeds: 1 cup = 140g

Oats, old fashioned rolled:
   1 cup = 90g

Oats, steel-cut: 1 cup = 140g

Peanut butter, smooth and
   crunchy: 1 cup = 240g

Peas, frozen: 1 cup = 130g

Pecans: 1 cup = 120g

Potatoes, mashed: 1 cup = 215g

Pretzels: 1 cup = 120g

Raisins: 1 cup = 160g

Sour cream: 1 cup = 240g

Spinach: 1 cup = 30 grams

Sugar, dark brown, packed:
   1 cup = 240g

Sugar, granulated or caster:
   1 cup = 200g

Sugar, icing (powdered):
   1 cup = 120g

Sugar, light brown, packed:
   1 cup = 220g

Sugar, light muscovado, packed:
   1 cup = 220g

Sultanas: 1 cup = 160g

Tomato ketchup: 1 cup = 225g

Walnuts: 1 cup = 100g

INDEX

ACKNOWLEDGMENTS

This cookbook couldn't have come together without the help, support—and appetites—of my family, friends, and colleagues.

Thank you to my editor Hilary VandenBroek who came up with the idea of this book and who had the vision and drive to see it through. It's testament to her faith and belief in the project that we've managed to have an incredibly productive transatlantic working relationship. I'm waiting for the day—hopefully soon!—when we can have a pint together in Ireland.

I'm grateful to copyeditor Jessica Easto for her eagle eye and ability to spot US / Ireland inconsistencies. All Jessica's work has undoubtedly made this a better book.

Thank you to my agent Sharon Bowers for being a font of sage advice and ever-entertaining emails.

Many thanks to Guinness Archive Manager Eibhlin Colgan, a fellow UCC graduate, who generously shared so much of her knowledge, and resources.

Thanks to Chef Sean Hunter at the Guinness Storehouse in Dublin, Executive Chef Kevin McCarthy, and Executive Sous-Chef Kamryn Dudley from the Open Gate Brewery in Baltimore for their recipes, time, and expertise.

I could not have put this book together without the assistance of all the team at Insight Editions. Kudos to photographer Evi Abeler, who took dishes that were developed in the gloom and darkness of a COVID winter and brought them to glorious, light-filled life.

Most of all, an enormous thank you to my family, who had to taste and rate a lot of beer-focused cooking and baking. As all this happened in the middle of the homeschooling / working-from-home phase of a pandemic, it meant that there was no escape whatsoever. I'm grateful for your patience, the critical (sometimes a little *too* critical) feedback, and your ever-willing tastebuds. Love, always.

ABOUT THE AUTHOR

Journalist, broadcaster, and writer Caroline Hennessy is the chair of the Irish Food Writers' Guild and a Ballymaloe Cookery School graduate. The co-author of *Sláinte: The Complete Guide to Irish Craft Beer and Cider* (New Island), she holds an M.Phil. in Irish History from University College Cork and is an experienced freelance journalist, focusing on food, drink, and travel since 2005. Caroline has won several awards at Bibliocook.com, regularly contributes to and develops recipes for a variety of publications, and is also an experienced public speaker, chairing and speaking at food and drink-focused debates and events.

She lives in a renovated 19th-century cottage in North Cork, Ireland, with a Kiwi, two small girls, a pair of cats, and three hens. www.bibliocook.com.

TITAN
BOOKS

144 Southwark Street
London SE1 0UP

www.titanbooks.com

f Find us on Facebook: www.facebook.com/titanbooks
🐦 Follow us on Twitter: @TitanBooks

All rights reserved. Published by Titan Books, London, in 2021.

A CIP catalogue record for this title is available from the British Library.

ISBN: 978-1-78909-817-4

Publisher: Raoul Goff
VP of Licensing & Partnerships: Vanessa Lopez
VP of Creative: Chrissy Kwasnik
VP of Manufacturing: Alix Nicholaeff
Editorial Director: Vicki Jaeger
Editor: Hilary VandenBroek
Production Editor: Jennifer Bentham
Senior Production Manager: Greg Steffen
Senior Production Manager, Subsidiary Rights: Lina s Palma

Photo Art Direction & Design: Amy C. King
Photography: Evi Abeler
Food Stylist: Paul Grimes
Prop Stylist: Paige Hicks

Special thanks to Warren Buchanan for everything he did
to help make this book a reality.

ROOTS of PEACE   🌳 REPLANTED PAPER

Insight Editions, in association with Roots of Peace, will plant two trees for each tree
used in the manufacturing of this book. Roots of Peace is an internationally renowned
humanitarian organization dedicated to eradicating land mines worldwide and
converting war-torn lands into productive farms and wildlife habitats. Roots of Peace
will plant two million fruit and nut trees in Afghanistan and provide farmers there with
the skills and support necessary for sustainable land use.

Manufactured in China by Insight Editions

10 9 8 7 6 5 4 3 2 1